The

LION

in the

Cubicle

By Chad Nash and Joe Lipman

Limits of Liability and Disclaimer of Warranty

The author and publisher shall not be liable for your misuse of this material. This book is strictly for informational and educational purposes.

Warning—Disclaimer

The purpose of this book is to educate and entertain. The author and/or publisher do not guarantee that anyone following these techniques, suggestions, tips, ideas, or strategies will become successful. The author and/or publisher shall have neither liability nor responsibility to anyone with respect to any loss or damage caused, or alleged to be caused, directly or indirectly by the information contained in this book.

ISBN-13: 978-0-9964048-9-1

Acknowledgments

I want to thank everyone who has shared part of my journey with me, starting with my mother, Brenda, and father, Gary, who raised me with Midwestern values that have carried me throughout my life. I would like to thank my brother, Scott Nash, and sister, LaDonna Jekot, who are not only some of my biggest fans, but also my greatest teachers. I would like to thank Sam Hart, Mat Jekot, Madeline Jekot, and Nash Jekot for the unconditional love and support along my many paths throughout the years.

I want to thank Nathan Roberts for 12 amazing years. Nathan, you reminded me how to feel and are very much one of the most significant influences in my life to date.

I would like to thank all my family back at Jack Henry & Associates including Russell Scritchfield, Rick Long, Sean Everhart, Cindy Bennight, and all three of my butterflies: Lynn, Peggy, and Tina. The chapters of this book have the JHA family all over. Russell, you helped created one of the pathways in my life that opened the biggest doors for my life.

At times there are moments in your life where friendships and bonds are created that mean more than at other times in your life. I want to thank those beautiful seeds from those friendships, for I am extremely greatly for their love and support. I want to thank Travis Richey and family, Brandon Levie, Jules Taggart, Mike Paganelli, Patrick Czar, Evan Tando, Joe Lipman, Ali Meza, Shawn Erdman, Coach Ryan, Kristi Kolby, Osvaldo Blackaller and family, and all of my friends back in San Diego.

I want to thank the countless years and hours from the staff at Data Springs including Candace Santos, Ryan Bakerink, and David To.

During the duration of writing this book I was helped by countless individuals whom I want to thank, including Greg Reid, Charles Vest, Patrick Carney, and all members or past members of the YES Mastermind. I want to thank Donna Kozik for being my big sister throughout this process and keeping me on track. Without you I am not sure what year this book would be published!

I want to thank Danny Tirado for supporting my kookoo-ness with a smile and several ups and down during the beginning to the end of this chapter in my life.

Online Resources

There are plenty of exercises, online resources, and a community of other lions waiting for you at www.InnerLion.com/BookResources.

Contents

Foreword

By Greg S. Reid

Those who know me know I love playing poker. I also enjoy teaching people how to play poker; the game is fun but it can also teach us much about life. There's an abundance of quotes out there, all variations on the theme: *You play the hand you're dealt.* In poker, as in life. You don't get to choose the cards you're dealt, but you certainly get to choose what you're going to do with them. Nor do you get to have a say in everything that life throws at you, but you absolutely have the final say when it comes time to deal with the situation.

I taught my friend Chad Nash how to play poker one summer. He was a natural and picked up the game quickly. The following summer I'd find myself in a poker tournament, last man standing. Some veterans that I'd played against and lost to had long since folded, and there I was, going head-to-head against the kid I'd just taught how to play the game a year ago. Yet poker is more than a game; it is a skill. And Chad had been implementing many of these skills in his life long before I ever came along and dealt him those five cards. And wouldn't you know? Chad beat me that day.

YOU MIGHT BE asking yourself why you should read yet another book aimed at self-improvement; there are already so many out there. To say the market is saturated is an understatement at best; yet, if you're like many people out there, you have yet to find what you are truly looking for among the overflowing bookshelves. You want something that is going to resonate, something that is going to speak directly to the core of your being. Even if some of the concepts are not familiar, you will be able to integrate them seamlessly into your life.

Chad Nash and Joe Lipman have written such a book that you now happen to be holding in your hands. Though they come from vastly different backgrounds, these two men have an innate understanding of how to take control of your own life and carve out exactly what you need in order to be fulfilled, financially, physically, emotionally, mentally. They examine, deconstruct, and explain how your thought patterns, longstanding beliefs, energy vibrations, and life experiences all contribute to how you think, feel, and act in the present, and how to go about modifying these things in order to change how you will be in the future. Both of these men knew from a young age what they wanted to do, though that doesn't necessarily mean it was a straight shot in getting them there. Many people find themselves in a similar situation, yet they are forced to put these desires on the back burner because they feel they simply don't have the tools needed to make the changes they need. If you are one of these people, you will recognize your struggle in Chad's and Joe's; you might find comfort that you are going through something similar and inspiration that you as well can do what it takes to live the life you have always wanted to live, the life you were meant to live.

Introduction

Imagine a lion. See its sleek, tawny coat, its compact, streamlined muscles. It is a regal, powerful animal, considered the king of all beasts, for good reason. Though not the biggest of the large cats—that title goes to the Siberian tiger—the lion is one of the most revered. Lions possess the ability to be both fierce and mellow. Their roar can be heard up to five miles away. In the wild, they spend up to 20 hours a day resting. Yet when it comes time to hunt or to protect their pride or territory, the lion can be one of the most fearsome animals out there. An angry lion is not something that you would want to be confronted with.

Compare that now to a smaller animal, something meek—say, a mouse, or maybe a hamster. An angry hamster is not something that would likely faze you. You might even find yourself wondering if an animal like a hamster is even capable of getting angry. A hamster is a small, timid creature that gives off a nervous, high-frequency energy that is easy to tune out or ignore. It spends the majority of its time running around and around on its little hamster wheel. A lion's energy, on the other hand, is strong and unmistakable. It is impossible to turn your back on it.

People can internalize the energetic characteristics of any animal. How many times have you heard a brave, protective mother referred to as a "mama bear"? Referring to people in animal terms is a very common practice and often helps paint a clearer picture of just what image we are trying to convey.

All things vibrate with energy. We are vibrational beings. This vibration can be subtle and almost undetectable except to the most experienced practitioner, or it may be extremely strong and undeniable. Some people may have a hard time believing that such energy exists, as it is not something that can readily be seen. Children understand vibrations more than adults do, as they know even without words when their mom or dad is angry and upset. Animals are also more in tune with vibrations and know in advance events about to occur. Have you ever had someone walk in the room and you could immediately feel the energy shift? An easy way to experience the tangibility and existence of this energy is to sit with your hands cupped, almost touching. Close your eyes and take a few deep breaths. Sit like this for as long as you'd like; soon you will start to feel a tingling in your hands. Slowly pull your hands apart, an inch or so, and then slowly move them back. You will be able to feel a slight resistance. The joints in your fingers will feel springy. This is energy—your energy.

Being aware of the energy you possess and put out there will be immensely helpful in creating the sort of life you want. But like anything that is not nourished and taken care of, energy can stagnate and lose its power. Have you ever been around someone who you felt like sucked all the energy out of you? We've all probably met someone like that at some point or another. It's not anything concrete that you can put your finger on, but there is a definite shift, a depletion of sorts, and most likely, you wanted nothing more than to get away from that person.

Let's go back to the examples of the lion and the hamster. Which type of energy would you like to internalize? How would you like to come across to others, to your family, friends, co-workers? One animal shows up big, whether it's hunting wildebeest out on the Serengeti or sprawled out under the shade of an Acacia tree to escape the brutal midday heat. The other is shy, scurrying, and easy to miss unless you're looking for it.

A hamster is very content living in captivity, but a lion is a different story. Even at the nicest zoos, the most expansive animal sanctuaries, a lion is always going to crave its freedom. A lion is never going to want to stay in a cage; it will always be looking for a way out—a way to freedom. And though many of us might not consider ourselves lions, at least not yet, we have somehow become complacent with the cages we have found ourselves in. This might be a startling realization for some, yet the majority of people living today exist with a cage of their own making, without even realizing it. Instead of steel bars or a chain-link fence marking off the parameter, though, these cages exist within the confines of time, Monday through Friday, 8 to 5. Added up over years, that is a lot of time to spend in a cubicle, putting your own dreams and desires on the back burner, perhaps so far back now that you've forgotten what they were. I am here to tell you it does not have to be like that. You do not have to spend the rest of your working life within the confines of a cage. You can be the lion who found its way out of the cubicle.

Chapter 1

The Cul-De-Sac

I grew up in a small town in Missouri, at the end of a cul-de-sac. It's been said that if you were fortunate enough to grow up on one of these closed roads that you very well might have a different way of thinking about things. For me, I'd say that thought certainly holds true.

Cul-de-sacs bring to mind idyllic childhoods, late summer nights spent romping through the neighborhood, and a whole herd of kids, yelling, laughing, trying to stretch out the time before mothers came to the door to call them in for bed. There is something about life on a cul-de-sac that creates a peaceful environment for children—a safety, perhaps because the peace of mind it affords their parents in that there is unlikely to be any speeding cars and few unfamiliar vehicles. The way out is the way in, no other way around it. It creates an atmosphere of security, a feeling of family among neighbors, a tribe of free-roaming children. This was my reality for the first 12 years of my life.

I KNEW FROM a young age I wanted to be in business. I remember thinking, *There's just one president of the United States, and there might be just one of this guy or one of this other guy, but there's a lot of successful businesspeople.* It seemed to me that anyone who wanted to be successful in business could, as long as they went about it the right way.

My first business was a fairly typical one for that of a young boy: I mowed lawns in the summer and shoveled snow in the winter. Fortunately for me, living in Missouri meant there was no shortage of snow, so I found myself employed year-round.

"I'm going into business for myself," I told my dad one evening. "I start tomorrow; I'm mowing Mrs. Johnson's lawn."

"That's great," he said. "Do you have a lawn mower?"

I looked at him in surprise. I was 8 years old. Why would any 8-year-olds have their very own lawn mower? "Well, no," I said. "I was planning to use yours."

"Of course," Dad replied. "I rent it out for three dollars an hour."

He managed to keep a straight face for all of two seconds and then started laughing, as though he'd just told the funniest joke in the world. "You should really see your face," he said when his laughter finally subsided enough for him to speak. "You are welcome to use the lawn mower. But let this be your first lesson in business: There will be startup costs. I'll give you the family discount, though, and say this one's on the house."

Dad was very anti-services; he believed that services were destroying the economy and people should be able to do things like change their own oil or mow their own lawns. Even at that young age, I could see his point. Like all children, I was used to relying on someone else for certain things, and sometimes that wasn't much fun. Yet at the same time, I also knew there were plenty of people out there who did not share Dad's view, who did not want to or did not know how to change their own oil or mow the lawn. That was where I came in.

And so, the night before my first official day of working for myself, I received the first of many business lessons I would learn.

DAD ALSO HELPED me come up with my company's tagline, which was: "I'm not happy until you're happy." Genius, I know, though at the time it seemed pretty good. Luckily, it's rather difficult to enrage someone over the way the snow is shoveled out of the driveway or how their lawn is cut.

Instead of hurrying home to do homework or go hang out with friends, I'd drop my school stuff off and, if it was warm weather, go fetch Dad's mower from the garage and start making the rounds. In the summer, when school was out and I found myself with far more time on my hands, I extended my services to include pet care—mostly of the dog and cat variety, though there were a few fish tanks to monitor and even an African gray parrot that was capable of singing show tunes. A few of the neighborhood kids tried setting a lemonade stand up at the end of the street, but they didn't have clear signage and seemed more interested in drinking the product than actually selling it.

It was a good location, though, and I saw immediately that there was great potential.

"How much money have you guys made so far?" I asked them one day when I was pushing the mower back from the Allens'.

"Some," replied one of the kids, Shawn. He (not-so) covertly set the plastic cup of lemonade he was drinking down on the table. He shook an old Folgers coffee can and what sounded like less than a handful of change rattled around. "We haven't been out here that long," he added.

I smiled. They'd been out there when I'd pushed the mower past on my way to the Allens', and the Allens do not have a small yard.

"Can I give you a few pointers?" I asked.

Shawn hesitated, but the other two kids nodded. They weren't just sitting out there to work on their tans. They wanted to make some money.

"Okay," Shawn finally relented. "What else should we be doing?"

"The first thing you want to do is stop drinking all the lemonade."

"I didn't want it to go to waste."

"Of course not. But you want it not to go to waste because you're selling it to your customers, not drinking it yourself. If that's all you wanted to do, you could've just as easily stayed at home and not lugged all this stuff out here."

The other kids nodded. "I *told* you," one of them whispered.

"So that's the first thing you want to do. The second thing is get a better sign. A piece of paper with *Lemonade* written on it with a Bic pen isn't going to cut it. No one is even going to notice it, especially not from the road. I mean, I barely noticed it and I'm walking by, less than four feet away. If you want to attract business, you've got to let people know that you're here. And this is actually a very good location. You've got that going for you. See how the road curves there?" I pointed, about a hundred yards away. "That's good, because people are going to slow down to take the turn. So they're not going to be zooming by, and if you put the sign a little ways up there, they'll have plenty of time to decide that they're really thirsty and would like nothing more than a refreshing glass of lemonade."

Shawn appeared to be considering this. "You *do* kinda sound like you know what you're talking about," he said. "Those are good points."

"Just give it a try."

"I have leftover poster board from a school project at my house," one of the kids volunteered. He looked at me. "Would that work?"

"That's a start. Do you have some markers? 'Cause a ballpoint pen isn't going to do it."

"Yeah, I think I have some markers."

They dispersed, leaving Shawn to man the stand in

case any customers happened to pull over.

I mowed a few more lawns that day and helped one neighbor weed her garden. She paid me and also gave me a plate of chocolate chip cookies.

"It's refreshing to see a young man who has such an innate entrepreneurial spirit as you do," she said. "Enjoy the cookies, dear."

When I got home it was almost time for dinner. I washed up, and then pulled the wad of bills from my pocket. I counted it at the counter, and when Dad came in, he stood there and watched me.

"Looks like you made out pretty well," he said. "How much you got there?"

"Seventy-five." Not bad for a day's work. It wasn't the most I'd ever made, but it was close.

Dad nodded. "Nice work, Chad," he said. "And I know for a fact your business is living up to its tagline. Several people have made a point to come tell me how happy they've been with the services you've provided."

It felt good to hear. I was only 8 years old, but I was making my own money and the possibilities seemed endless.

I SPENT THE next few years mowing lawns and shoveling driveways. I added a paper route in, too, and I had also turned into something of a neighborhood consultant. After that first interaction with Shawn, kids would come to me and ask for help starting their own businesses. The girl across the street wanted to do something with the little doll clothes she made on her mom's sewing machine. Another wanted to start a babysitting service with a few of her friends. At that point, I had my own savings account, which I made deposits into regularly. I liked to see the balance grow, and I'd try to guess how high I could get it in a month, six months, a year.

But then, when I turned 12, my parents announced that we were moving, to a city called Independence. Dad was getting transferred there for work, and it was time to say goodbye to life on the cul-de-sac.

Our new house in Independence was smack in the middle of a busy thoroughfare, about as opposite from a cul-de-sac as you could get. You could hear the cars at all hours of the night, zooming down the road as though they had somewhere important to get to. There were barely any lawns, and, on my stretch of street, even less children. Mostly, it seemed like old people and their little lap dogs and decrepit cats. I started another paper route, but it was a lot less fun riding on the chaotic city streets than down the quiet roads in Blue Springs. The city took care of most of the snow removal, and what walkways I did shovel, the people seemed to think I was doing it to earn a Boy Scout merit badge. The flow of money going into my bank account started to dwindle. As my teenage years approached, I found myself with a lot more time on my hands. And that's when I started to get into other, less wholesome things.

Chapter 2

Belief Systems

I f the first half of my childhood was spent being very sociable and outgoing, the second half was spent in far more isolation, of the self-imposed sort. I got into computers.

For many people, a computer is an innocuous piece of machinery, but for me, it quickly became a place where my adventurous personality was able to find its way into bad things. Essentially, I became a hacker.

It was easy enough to disguise that sort of thing, to hide it from your parents. My parents had no idea what I was up to—they were busy with their lives and seemed glad that I had an interest in something. If either happened to peek into my room and see me hunched over my workstation, it was entirely feasible that I'd be working on a school assignment and not, say, hacking into various systems in order to sell calling cards.

Some people have the innate ability to follow rules, to do as they're told, and they might just live better lives because of it. For others, this might not be the case. If you are in possession of a certain type of spirit, a certain need to create, or explore, it will find its way out no matter what is done to try to constrain it.

I think this is why high school is so difficult for some, yet others can skate on by like it wasn't even a thing. Unless you're one of the fortunate souls that gets to go to a charter or some other alternative school, the rules of high school are pretty regimented, pretty standard, and everyone is pretty much expected to do the same thing. When you're in high school, the universe is very narrow and structured: Go to class, pay attention, do your homework, rinse and repeat for the next four years. Most teachers weren't interested in anything that deviated from their lesson plan.

So I poured my creative energies not into chemistry homework or English projects, but into computers, and in doing so I discovered a whole new world of possibilities, of ways to make money, of getting away with things that most people wouldn't even dream of. It started with fairly simple schemes—replicating the tone that a payphone hears once coins have been inserted so you could make all the calls you want without actually putting in any money; I cloned cell phones and had my own 900 number, which allowed me to go to various stores, ask to use their phone, then call my 900 number. At 25 dollars or more per call, it was an easy way to make a tidy sum of money all by just dialing a few digits. My parents were pleased that I had a burgeoning interest in computers and assumed that I was doing only benign things. Eventually

I got into hacking into systems and selling calling cards. This would prove to be the end of the line for those activities, and, at the age of 15, I was summoned by the Secret Service.

It was a day like any other, and I was in my bedroom at my desk, in front of my computers. Then the Secret Service came calling. If you've ever seen the '90s movie *Hackers* and can remember the scene when the Secret Service arrests one of the young hackers, you've got an approximate idea of how things went down that morning. They emptied everything out, took all of my computers, and went through every electrical box. I was cuffed, arrested, detained, and questioned. And though the Secret Service never actually charged me, it was definitely a wakeup call for my family and me.

Not long after I was released, Dad sat me down at the kitchen table. "This is not the sort of thing you want to do with your life," he said. "And I hope you realize that things could've turned out a whole lot worse."

I did, and yet, at the same time, I didn't. When you're a teenager, sitting in your room in front of your computer, the idea that something like the Secret Service busting in and arresting you and taking all your equipment seems very abstract. The sort of thing that might—*might*—happen to someone else, or to someone in a movie, but not actually in real life.

"Your mother and I have been doing a lot of talking," Dad continued. "And we've decided to move back to Blue Springs. At this point, I think it'd be better for everyone.

Think of this as your second chance, Chad. You're a smart kid and you've got a lot of potential, but you've got to use it the right way. You could really do some great things with your life, which probably won't happen if you end up in federal prison."

SO WE MOVED back to Blue Springs, and though I'd decided to be good after everything that happened with the Secret Service, I quickly found my resolve wavering. It's not that I wanted to be bad so much that creative energy is nearly impossible to keep under wraps. If you are truly passionate about something, it will find its way out over and over again. Even the Secret Service can't scare it away. And so, even though I'd resolved to be good, my junior and senior years were not without their share of detentions and suspensions. That energy had to go somewhere, and most of the time, my unwitting teachers were the recipients.

WHEN I WAS 17, I started my own company, a retail computer store ran out of my garage, with my childhood best friend, Dave. We'd build computers as well as upgrade people's existing computers, which was common practice in those days. And though it was just something that Dave and I started to have something to occupy our time with—something to keep us busy until we finally graduated high school—we ended up with a lot of business. KNBC news came and did a story on us, and the *Kansas City Star* did a front-page story. There we were, right on the front page of the newspaper. My parents bought many copies of the paper and sent them to all the relatives who wanted an issue. Mom had the article framed, and on more than one occasion I caught my dad looking at it, a smile on his face.

Dave and I learned a lot through that company, things like setting up the business, and the joys of sales tax and ordering products as a wholesaler. It was a good time, because we were doing things on our own terms, but luckily these terms happened to align with the government's idea of what is good and correct, and so, no more visits from the Secret Service. It seemed my creative energy had finally found a place to call home.

BUT AS ANYONE who owns their own business can surely attest, things get mighty stressful awful quick. I had just finished high school and thought that the stress would be gone, but it suddenly seemed magnified a thousand-fold. What was I supposed to do now? I didn't want to continue the company, even though it was doing well— the whole purpose to starting it was to have something to do while we were in school. Now we weren't, and now I was supposed to know what I was going to do, but I didn't. College seemed like the logical choice, since that's what most everybody else was doing, but since I hadn't actually applied to any, community college would be my only option.

Because our business had done so well, I had a lot of money(especially for a teenager) so I did the only thing I could think of: I went on a three-week vacation to Hawaii, certain that a respite in tropical paradise would be all that I needed to figure out exactly what it was I wanted to do with the rest of my life.

WHEN YOU LIVE somewhere like the United States, it's easy to forget that there are other ways of life—that there are people all over the world who do things much, much differently than we do things here. But in Hawaii, I met a lot of fellow travelers, from all over the world, who had a much different way of seeing things. While back in Missouri, people had raised their eyebrows when I told them I was taking a three-week vacation, to most of the people I met while staying in hostels, three weeks was nothing. I was shortchanging myself. Many had been traveling for months, and would continue to travel for months after that. For a little while, I assumed that I was merely in the company of the ultra-rich, people who could afford to travel to these luxury, paradise locations for the majority of the year. But after talking to some of these people, I realized that they were not. In fact, what I had budgeted for three weeks, many of those travelers could get by on for nine months. They didn't require a barrage of entertainment or four-star hotels or gourmet meals. Much of their time was spent relaxing on the beach, enjoying a slower way of life. Time itself, in fact, seemed to slow down, and it didn't matter when you woke up or went to bed. There was no need to check your watch or set an alarm or even give much thought to what day it was. Everything kind of ran together; you might be aware of the natural cycle of the sun and the moon, of light and dark, but that was about it. There was no need for calendars or wristwatches. It was so different from the way of life I was used to. And I loved it. The most stressful decision I had to make was whether I wanted to go swimming before breakfast or after. Some days, I did both. I let my return ticket expire, and I stayed for another three months.

I could hear the concern in people's voices when I called home to let them know not to expect me back when they originally thought they would.

"Is everything okay?" my mother asked, as though me telling her I was extending my stay was actually code for "gotten into trouble with the law again."

"Everything is great!" I told her. "I'm having an amazing time and I just really feel like I'm supposed to stay out here a while longer."

"Well...what are you *doing* out there?"

Going to the beach, eating delicious food, meeting all sorts of interesting people. These were all things I'd done and would continue to do, but to my mother, I replied, "Getting life experience." The answer seemed to satisfy her, though she did end the call by asking if I planned to come back after the three months, in a tone that suggested she didn't actually believe I would.

And for those three months, time really didn't exist, and money certainly wasn't a concern, and *making* money really wasn't a concern, because that's not what that lifestyle was all about. You exist in this kind of beautiful, gauzy, haze, where it's almost like a dream, all the time. And you think to yourself, *Gee, this is a dream I hope I never wake up from.* And some people never do, and they are completely content. For a period of time, I certainly believed I was one of those people. But then one day I noticed a feeling that I hadn't noticed before—this pull, really, to go back to Missouri. To go to college, to get my degree, because I knew it was something that was important to my parents.

So I left Hawaii, and went back to Missouri, where things of course, did not go anywhere near as planned.

Chapter 3

Adventures in College

When I returned from Hawaii, I enrolled at the local community college and got a job as a technician at the cable company. I could tell my parents were pleased that I was both enrolled in school and gainfully employed, as opposed to living the beach bum existence in tropical paradise, and though I knew I was doing the right thing, there was definitely a period of adjustment when I longed to be back on the back on the North Shore of Oahu.

For a little while, my life fell into a fairly stable and predictable routine: I had my work schedule, and though the job was fairly mundane, it wasn't the worst; and then I had my classes, and like the job, it was not the most enthralling experience, but it was okay.

Who knows for how long that routine might have continued, but eventually, I got fired from the job. I had switched to a night shift and had taken to watching a movie or two to help pass the time. Things were just slower on the night shift, and since my boss had suggested

I might use the slow time to do some homework, I figured watching a movie would be an acceptable way to
pass a few hours.

Unfortunately, my boss didn't agree, and I was fired. It
would've been more upsetting but it seemed like the perfect opportunity to enroll at a four-year college, seeing as
I already had two years of community college under my
belt at that point.

In some ways, I had the normal college experience:
I took classes, hung out with friends, tried to figure out
exactly what it was that I wanted to get a degree in. A
few of my peers seemed to have a clear and direct idea
of what they were doing and where they were going, but
most of the other students seemed more interested in par-
tying and having a good time. In fact, more often than
not, many of them would justify their hard-partying ways
with the hard and fast belief that college was the final
hurrah, the last gasp of freedom, unfettered youth, before
being tethered to some job—to an adult way of life.

The summer between my sophomore and junior years
of college I was back in Blue Springs, and I overheard a
lot of talk around town from kids my age, generally along
the lines of this:

Kid 1: My parents are really after me to get a good job.

*Kid 2: I know. I think I walked into every store down-
town last week and asked if they were hiring.*

*Kid 1: Me too. It would be great if there was some other
way to get your information out there. It's exhausting,
going to all those places.*

Kid 2: And none of them ever seem to call back.

I heard variations of that same conversation and I started thinking: Was there some other way that people could get their resumes out there to potential employers? What if it was as simple as signing up on a website and uploading a cover letter and resume? All I'd need was a database of potential employers, which I could then have the cover letters and resumes e-mailed to. In order to procure a large enough list to make the website possible, I'd need to raise some funds. So I went around and asked all of my friends and friends' parents if they were interested in investing in the company. Most of them were, and together we formed what was called a Missouri partnership.

AFTER THE JOB Guys, I developed a piece of software called Resume Blowout, which was a desktop application and you'd run through a wizard that would ask about your previous work experience, your education, and all your basic information, and then it would generate a resume for you. I included a few generic resumes as samples, which ended up being a rather large learning lesson for me because I ended up getting sued by another resume company because of those generic samples.

There's a lot that goes into any business venture, whether it's starting your own electrical company or developing a piece of software. I was young, so it's easy enough to say it didn't even occur to me that using a sample so similar to theirs would be illegal. The very idea of being sued by this company, though, seemed silly to me.

Didn't they realize I was just a kid? I was 21 years old doing this out of my dorm room. Did they expect to receive a settlement in Ramen noodles and term papers? Because I had plenty of those and not much of anything else—certainly not the vast sum they were looking for. Perhaps naively, I figured it could all be cleared up by relaying the information that I was just a student, not some big company with deep pockets that could handle that kind of thing. But the people at the other company didn't want to hear it, or didn't get it—or knew, rather, that just because *I* was in college and didn't have a lot in my name, I was joint and several liability with the friends and parents of friends who had originally invested with me. We were not incorporated, there was no separate entity. Money for the settlement would not have to come from just me; all the people who invested were also on the hook, and I felt terrible. An oversight on my part had ramifications for people who had only wanted to help me out—who had believed in what I was doing and wanted to be supportive. They had not signed up for this. Yet there they were, having to use money they had set aside for remodeling their house or helping their kids out in school, or going on a well-deserved vacation, to hire a lawyer.

It was difficult for all of us to believe the company would still want to go through with the lawsuit once they realized we were not the big business they thought we were. I took a $50,000 judgment against me, though I tried one last time to plead my case and I called the guy from the other resume company.

"I don't have $50,000," I told him. "I'm in college. I'm basically a broke college student, so there's no way I can afford to pay you what you want."

"We can put you on a monthly payment plan," the guy said, sounding incredibly pleased at his generosity. "How does that sound? I know you need to live and make money, so why don't we set up some sort of monthly plan?"

"What if I gave you $5,000? I could get that much together."

He laughed. "Are you giving me a choice between $5,000 and $50,000? Hmm, hold on. Let me think about that for a minute."

We got off the phone shortly thereafter. He wanted $50,000, and he wasn't going to accept anything else. To him, it didn't matter where it came from, or how I went about getting it, as long as it ended up in his account. My parents tried to act like they thought everything was going to be okay, but I could see how stressed they were about it. I knew they'd help me out any way they could, but $50,000 is a lot of money, and I didn't want them to feel like they would have to re-mortgage the house or forego any chance of retirement just to get me out of the mess I'd gotten myself into.

So, the day after I graduated college, I filed bankruptcy.

I hadn't realized the full weight of the stress of the lawsuit—of feeling responsible for the effects that it had on the lives of the people who had invested in me—until I was finally free of it. I was no longer shackled to this

50-thousand-pound weight. Instead, I had the opportunity for a fresh start. Like getting fired from the technician job had ushered in the opportunity to go to college full-time, filing bankruptcy wiped the slate clean and filled me with hope and inspiration to really get out there and *do* something. While there was the literal, physical act of filing for bankruptcy, it was also symbolic in that it helped release the negative energy associated with the whole thing. Only in getting rid of certain energies, do you allow yourself to make room for new, positive energy. You are not doing anyone any favors by staying within your circle of doom. This can be hard to realize at first, because change can be difficult to make, and though negative energy might be draining or make you feel bad, if it's what you've grown accustomed to, it is easy to let yourself stagnate in it. It is easy to succumb to it and not be able to see a way out. But often, it's making that first change that is the hardest, when the energy is most reluctant to shift. Imagine trying to push a boulder. It's going to require a lot of effort to initially get the thing moving, but once you do, it gets easier. You build momentum, and if you keep up with it, you might realize at some point that it feels like you're hardly doing anything at all.

I'd felt mired in the muck of getting sued and of the lawsuit, but I was free of that, I had a degree, and I was determined to take what I had learned from the whole thing and get out there and do something.

Chapter 4

Lion in the Cubicle

I ended up getting a job about an hour away from Springfield as a computer programmer. It was a good job at a large corporation and I decided going in there that I was going to be more than just an employee. I really wanted to prove myself, not just to my bosses and co-workers, but also to my parents, friends, and myself.

"How is the job going?" Mom asked me one day. Though I wasn't working at Hy-Vee, she was pleased that I was gainfully employed and receiving a regular paycheck.

"It's okay," I said. "The commute can be kind of brutal."

The commute was about to get a lot more brutal, though at the time I didn't realize it. Winter comes fast and cold in the Midwest, and we were only a few days into it when the heater in my Jeep quit working. The Jeep had a soft-top and, though there were no noticeable gaping holes in it, I might as well have been driving without it; it felt so cold. I took to wearing my parka, hat, gloves, and even a ski mask on the coldest days. Imagine the looks people gave me when they drove past me with a ski mask on!

Perhaps it was that winter commute with no heat that was the final straw, but I knew I had to get out of the Midwest, and soon. It was time. But I had this good job and I didn't want to just up and quit. So I started thinking and one day, I went in to talk to my boss, Richard.

Our company had just purchased another company in San Diego, and it seemed to me that it would be a good idea to have a guy or two from the main office there. I had already been working there over eight months and proven myself a value to the company. I gave Richard an ultimatum and I didn't leave much room for discussion. I simply stated that because of family reasons I needed to move to San Diego right away, and if they wanted me to continue to work for them, this was the only direction for me—I was moving with or without the job. In my e-mail I offered this as a "trial" that could last a year and I would agree to come back. It took two days before Richard called me into his office, and I was extremely scared during that time.

"Family reasons?" Richard said. He looked at me with an eyebrow raised. "You'd be willing to come back after a year?"

Okay, so maybe I lied. There were a few lessons here though because that lie about family would later become a running joke in my department and everyone every day would ask me about my family because they knew it wasn't true. At the time I felt stuck though and I did what

I felt I had to do. To date, I don't believe if I treated the situation with a direct request and ultimatum it would have been approved. Another lesson, and an even more important lesson, is that when you offer companies or bosses a "trial" version, then they always have a way out and are more likely to allow you to pursue what you are asking for.

"OKAY, WE WILL announce this at the next department meeting," Richard said.

I refrained from jumping out of my chair and across his desk to give him a hug and instead just smiled calmly. "You are willing to return after one year?" Richard asked.

"Yes," I said. "This is a great company to work for and I think that I could easily return after a year." I knew I had no plans of returning, and I think Richard did, too.

"Well, Chad, you've been an exemplary employee and you're certainly an asset to this company. We'd be happy to do this for you." I did it. My plan worked.

AND SO, I found myself getting ready to move, not just out of the Midwest, but also out of the cubicle. Notice, though, how it didn't all happen at once; I didn't just go in there and say, "*Hey, Richard, I'd like to start working from home all the time.*" Especially when you're just beginning to transition away from the cubicle, you want to start with small steps. Ask if you can work from home every other Friday on a trial basis. Or ask if you can even just work some mornings from your home office because of personal reasons. Once the company realizes you are just as productive at home, they will reward you with more freedom gradually.

The company helped me out with some of my moving expenses, and life in San Diego was good. Not all corporations are bad, not all view their employees as dispensable drones, and this company that I was working for was a good example of that. And for some people, if you do happen to find yourself at one of these corporations, where they treat you well and you enjoy what you're doing, you might be perfectly content to stay where you are. At the end of each day, you might go home happy and fulfilled. If this is you, great. For a lot of people, though, this is not the case.

It can be rather disconcerting, actually. Here you are, with a good-paying job, that you don't hate, and you might even have a boss you can get along with, yet there is something inside of you that is restless, that is not content, that is certain there is something else out there, and that you'd be able to find it if only you knew what it was or how to go after it. If this situation sounds familiar, you might also find yourself dealing with feelings of guilt. You have a job, after all, and maybe one that even pays pretty well, which is more than some people can say. Shouldn't you be grateful? Shouldn't you just accept this and try to ignore those feelings of discontentment?

People have a number of ways of doing this. They take up hobbies, they work harder, they look forward to their next vacation, they anticipate a raise. All these things, though, are merely a temporary fix, a Band-Aid of sorts, over a symptom that might require something closer to surgery to eradicate it. So even though I knew that the company I was working for was a good one, I also knew that I wouldn't be staying there forever. I stayed for about two years, during which time I decided I wanted to have another stream of income as well, so I started a company, which my brother helped me name, called Data Springs. While I was creating my website, I used a platform that had just come out called Dot Net Nuke, which was a shared, open source platform. As I used Dot Net Nuke, I started building things I needed into my own website. When you're identifying your own needs and meeting them in ways that you're having to contribute to, that's very often how you come up with ideas for what you want to do in your business. Even though I was still employed with the other company, still in my cubicle—though that cubicle had been transplanted to San Diego—I was able to simultaneously be working to get out of the corporate environment.

So where are you on this journey? Perhaps you're just starting out—just realizing that there is something more for you out there than within the confines of your cubicle. You might want to consider asking other people who have worked there for any length of time for tips or suggestions, or even just how they like their job. Try asking them if they would rather have an extra month off than an increase in pay after a year. Most people will probably say they'd like the raise. But what about three years? Or five, 10, or 15? As the years begin to add up, it's easier to realize how entrapped you can be by your job, regardless of the amount of raises or other perks that happen to be thrown in. I like to think of these perks as *cage treats.* They're the things that corporations offer up to entice you to stay and make you feel comfortable in your cage. They offer you a raise, or they offer you a new benefit or maybe a new position. And everyone loves a treat, so of course you're going to take it. You work hard, after all. You deserve it. Just be aware of what it is and don't forget that you are still in that cage.

You might find yourself wondering if there's a way to take advantage of the treat without harm. It's easy to start thinking of the nice vacation or new laptop or wardrobe you might spring for now that you have a raise. Or maybe a better television, or a new patio set, even though the one you currently have is perfectly fine. There's no deny-ing that material things are nice, and that buying yourself something every once in a while is a fine reward in and of itself, but you'll find yourself running into trouble if every time you have a little extra income, whether it's from a raise or a bonus, you're spending it on something that is only going to provide you with temporary happiness. So just be aware of this, because the path out of the cubicle can become exponentially longer with new mortgages, car payments, boat payments, and all the other upkeep their monthly treats require.

MOVING TO SAN Diego was not just good for helping

me get out of the cubicle; I also met some amazing people—two in particular. The first of these is Joe Lipman, who co-authored this book. Though Joe and I come from vastly different backgrounds, meeting him was like being re-introduced to an old friend. We were kindred spirits, and it was refreshing to have someone in my life who shared a similar philosophy and outlook and had pretty much since childhood.

The second person I actually met one day after I got done hanging out with Joe: Jason White, an East Coast transplant. He was in his late 20s, and we started talking while standing in line at the coffee shop. When I met Joe, he'd long since escaped the cubicle and was doing just fine working for himself. Jason, however, had only just started his journey. Both of these men knew, from an early age, that they wanted something more, and though they went about different ways of getting it, in the end, both found great success in freeing their inner lion.

Chapter 5

Freedom

When you move to a new place, there is no better feeling than meeting someone you immediately hit it off with. Within the first few minutes of being around Joe, I knew he was such a person. It didn't take long for us to start hanging out on a regular basis, and as we got to know each other better, it became clear that, though we had very different upbringings, we were cut from the same cloth.

JOE GREW UP in Coronado, California, which, if you're not familiar with the area, is a popular tourist destination and well-known for its luxurious beachfront hotels. Basically, Joe grew up in paradise, in a place where the kids spent their summers hanging on the beach and having a good time, not working summer jobs. If they needed money, they asked their parents. Getting a fancy Mercedes sports car to celebrate your 16th year on earth was not an uncommon occurrence in Joe's circle of friends. When he told me this, I tried to imagine such a thing happening in Blue Springs. Yeah, right.

"So what'd you end up with for your sweet sixteen?" I asked. "Did you go for the SLK or maybe the Audi TT?"

Joe smiled. "Neither. Actually, I think I was working on my 16th birthday. I always knew I wanted to have my own money, from a very early age, even though all my friends were very content to just ask Mom and Dad when they needed more cash. Not that my parents wouldn't have given me the money—they had no problem with it; it's just something I didn't feel right asking for. Having my own money meant I wouldn't have to go to them for it. It meant I had done something to earn it, which was important. I wanted the freedom that came with being in charge of yourself. Even as a kid."

That much was apparent. When he was 8, Joe decided to start his own golf ball sales company. And when the Coronado Municipal Golf Course is practically your backyard, it seemed like perfect opportunity. He figured there would certainly be no shortage of people who needed golf balls.

"I'd get the wheelbarrow out of the shed and wheel it down to the course, where I'd fill it up with balls and then bring them back home. I wasn't too concerned with things like obtaining a permit or whatever other permission would've been required to do what I was doing. The only person whose permission I was really after was my mom's, and that was so I could use her washing machine to get the balls sparkling clean and ready for sale."

I cringed, thinking of my own mother's reaction if her washing machine were to be used for anything other than dirty clothes and linens.

"My mom wasn't thrilled about it," Joe said, smiling at the memory. "I actually remember quite clearly that she arrived home right around the time the golf balls entered the final spin cycle. She looked toward the laundry room, then to me, then back to the laundry room, and wanted to know if her washing machine was about to explode. I assured her it wasn't and told her what I was doing. I think she found the whole thing somewhat amusing and maybe a little inconvenient. She did make me agree to buy her a new washing machine if I broke hers. But the machine actually did a great job getting those golf balls cleaned up. Then, I'd load them back into the wheelbarrow and take them outside, where I'd yell to the golfers as they crossed the street to the course. *Buy golf balls from me!* The first couple people probably did so out of pity more than anything else, seeing this kid there with a wheelbarrow full of golf balls, but once others started seeing people doing it, they wanted to, too."

While business was never exactly booming for Joe, he found himself with more and more customers each day. He saved all his money and began to plan exactly what he would do with it. Could he expand operations? Offer more than just golf balls? Listening to Joe relive this story reminded me in so many ways of my own experience back in Blue Springs. It was like Joe and I had been on identical trajectories—him in California, me in Missouri.

The concluding part of Joe's story just solidified this idea even more. The doorbell rang one afternoon and he answered it to find none other than one of Coronado's finest standing there on the front stoop.

"He wanted to know if I was Joe Lipman," Joe said. "I remember staring up at him. He was wearing these aviator shades, so I was reflected back—this tiny little image of myself. He had a really stern look on his face, and I was suddenly overcome with the certainty that he was going to haul me off to jail. But he didn't. He just asked if my parents were home. My mom was not amused when she saw who was at the door and he told her that what I was doing was illegal. Which, as it turns out, I was. You can't conduct private business on public land. I needed to have certain permits, and, there had been a few complaints. So I agreed to stop, though I wasn't going to stop right away. I needed to have at least one more day of business."

As Joe told me this story, I wondered how many kids, maybe at that very moment, were getting reprimanded for wanting to be their own boss—for wanting the freedom to earn something on their own. Think of the message that sends: *Don't be creative. Don't try to do something outside the box. Do what is expected of you, what is safe.* Indoctrinating children with that way of thinking is simply paving the way right into the cubicle. And for Joe, this is exactly what happened.

On his last day of business as a golf ball salesman, he was approached by a man named Travis who had heard a lot about Joe and what Joe was doing. He had heard, in fact, that this young man had been approached by the police about no longer conducting this particular business, yet there he was, still doing exactly that. Travis told him that when his buddy finished relaying the story about this kid selling golf balls, the first thing he thought was, *I want that kid to work for me. I want the type of sales guy that just doesn't back and down and doesn't give up.* Of course, Joe was only 8 years old at the time, and if it was illegal for him to sell golf balls then it was certainly illegal for him to go work for this man, who owned a technology company. Still, Travis passed along his business card, which Joe kept tucked in a shoebox that he kept on a shelf in his closet.

"I forgot about that card for a long time," Joe said. "And then, when I was in college, I decided I needed to get a job—because again, even though I was taking a full course load and my parents were more than happy to help out, I didn't want to take their money. So I found that business card, one weekend when I went home to visit, and I called Travis, who remembered me pretty much right away, even though a decade had passed."

"Clearly you made an impression," I said. And conversely, Travis had made an impression on Joe. If you are lucky, you will always have people in your life who want to offer you support, but unfortunately for many, this is not the norm. It is easier to doubt, to be negative, or to just have a complete lack of interest. So when you come across people who *will* offer you support, whether it's someone close to you or someone you just meet in passing, really listen to what he or she has to say. Though his conversation with Joe on his last day of business had been a brief one, Travis had offered Joe support and encouragement. Joe remembered this, and because of that, 10 years later, their paths would cross again.

"He asked me to come down for a job interview, and basically hired me on the spot," Joe said. "And I was excited about the job. Selling super computers. I didn't know much about super computers—yet—but that was okay. I had always been good at adapting and learning as I went. I would be making my own money; I was going to be responsible for myself."

But what Joe did not realize, at least at first, was that by accepting the job, he was stepping right into the lion's cage (the cubicle).

I'M SURE YOU'RE familiar with the tale of the Little Red Hen. The hen does all the work, and, in the end, she reaps the rewards. Joe found out that life in the cubicle is pretty much exactly like that, until you get to the end. In the cubicle world, those who do the hard work are seldom rewarded as they should be. Re-imagine the Little Red Hen, except change the ending and have it so the barnyard animals, who did nothing to help, get to eat the bread she has made. Maybe she gets a few crumbs, if she's lucky. This is not the sort of story you'd want to hear, or read to your kids. This is not the type of moral lesson we want to perpetuate, is it? So why, then, do so many of us find ourselves in that exact situation?

Joe found himself putting considerable effort into finding lucrative opportunities that he'd then have to pass off to a higher-level sales guy who would be the one to close the deal. That guy would receive the commission while Joe got paid just above minimum wage. Regardless of what you're doing—whether it's selling super computers or bathing dogs—it doesn't feel good to be the one who puts in most of the effort and is given only a fraction of the reward. It just doesn't.

Joe continued to work there, though, and he was able to amass his own clientele while he built relationships, not just with the customers, but the vendors as well. He stayed at the job for nearly 10 years, during which time they doled out a number of cage treats, like a larger office and pay increases. But essentially, he was still trapped. The job required he stay within certain margins and meet specific goals each week. There was always the possibility of getting canned if he did not meet these expectations. Joe felt like he was working incredibly hard, yet he was never really happy.

"I never woke up eager to get to work. I never looked forward to going in there. And so the logical question would be: Why stay? Why continue to do something that is negatively affecting how you feel?"

For Joe, it was the same reason as so many other people. There are bills, responsibilities, and the comfort of staying with what you know, what you're used to, even if it's not exactly what you want. It's easy to get into a rut—into a comfort zone that actually isn't so comfortable.

Eventually, as the stresses of his job mounted, Joe decided he needed some distance, he needed some downtime to reassess what he was doing and try to figure out how he could be doing it differently.

"That can be a really hard first step to make," I said. "Just deciding that you need to reevaluate things. Because it's so easy to feel overwhelmed with everything, especially when a solution doesn't seem readily available."

"Exactly," Joe said. "And it had taken me a long time to get there. But I'd reached my wit's end. Something had to change. This wasn't how life was supposed to be. I took a trip to Mexico, had plenty of time to think, and when I came back, I gave my notice at my job."

Joe took the relationships he'd cultivated with the vendors and customers, and, with a partner, started Advanced HPC. He and his business partner were able to design a successful company with employees who work *with* them, because they all work together as a team.

He says, "It's important to me that anyone who works for me feels like they have the level

of freedom that they can go on vacation whenever they wanted, that they can make as much—or as little—money as they wanted to. I wanted my employees to feel like they had control over their working lives, so we implemented a commission-only structure. In other words: If you don't work, you don't get paid. If you work a lot, you'll get paid a lot. The hope was that this sort of structure would inspire people to work and continue to inspire them to do well when they saw the benefit of their hard work paying off.

"One of the goals in my career is to solve problems and to also help people out. I know I'm not the only one out there who feels like this, and I like to tell my story to people because I think, on some level, they'll find it relatable. For a while, I stayed stuck in a situation that was making me chronically unhappy because I was fearful of the change that would be required to better my situation. I was a lion who was trapped in a cubicle for a long, long time, yet there are people out there who have been trapped even longer. This doesn't mean it's too late to get out! This doesn't mean that you can't start the business that you always wanted to, or find a job that will allow you freedoms your current one does not."

Joe's story could've gone a number of different ways, and his is a good example that your path to getting out of the cubicle is not always going to be a linear one, or a particularly short one. But Joe's innovative, entrepreneurial spirit is just as bright now as it was when he was a kid selling golf balls.

For many of us, childhood seems like a lifetime ago, but think back for a moment, if you will. I'm sure at some point you had a lemonade stand, or mowed lawns, or walked dogs, or watered your neighbors' plants while they were on vacation. Can you recall what it felt like to be paid for whatever task it was you'd completed? You were 8, 9, 10 years old, and you went out there and provided a service and were paid for it. It was a good feeling. It's easy enough to dismiss that initial feeling of accomplishment, of pride, to being young, to it being a first-time thing. You were just a kid, so of course getting some money of your own was exciting. Being paid for something you did imbued you with a feeling of worth. You didn't go out and ask your friend to let you work for him or her, tell you when to come in and how long to stay, and decide how much you were going to be paid. Whether you were pulling weeds for an elderly neighbor or shoveling the sidewalk, you were your own boss. That doesn't have to be the sort of thing you leave behind in childhood. You did it then, and you can still do it now.

Chapter 6

The Hy-Vee Mindset

There's a grocery store in Blue Springs called Hy-Vee, which is just like any other chain grocery store. It was a popular place for kids to work for the summer or after school. My best friend, Dave, got a job there, and I remember one day, my mother coming into my room and finding me at my workstation. I had just started the resume company, and she sat down at the edge of my bed and asked me what I was doing. I told her, and she sighed.

"Chad, I wish you could just get a good job," she said. "Something stable. Something where you could count on the paycheck every week. Doesn't that sound nice? One less thing to have to worry about. I know Dave's working at Hy-Vee. I bet they're still hiring. Why don't you go down there and fill out an application?"

In her mind, it was a perfectly legitimate question. My previous activities with computers had only resulted in trouble, and of course, like any parent, my mom wanted only what was best for me. But she had a different belief system, and in her mind, like many others', finding a stable job where you had a dependable paycheck was paramount to anything else. It can be a very common experience that your family or friends or those closest to you hold you back, though that is probably not their intention.

It can take some of the sting out, realizing that your spouse or parent or friend is not actually trying to hold you back because they don't want you to succeed; rather, they mistakenly believe that your path to success should conform to the ideas and beliefs they have been indoctrinated with.

This is not to say their ideas are wrong, per se. Many people hope to make it through college and get a good-paying job. This is what is instilled in the general population from an early age, and it's easy enough to look around and see that's what most of our peers are doing. Yet if you really stop to think about it, it is amazing that more people are not angry, or horrified, at the situation they've gotten themselves into. The lion inside you might feel flashes of discontentment, but they're easily written off as just part of life. But spending eight or nine or even more hours a day in a cubicle does *not* have to be your life.

Remember Jason White from Chapter 4? This was one of the very first things Jason and I talked about, sitting right outside of that coffee shop where we first met. He'd moved to San Diego from a coastal Maine town, the sort of place where rich people went to play for the summer and the locals busted their butts making sure the tourists were happy and spending money.

"That's not the sort of life I was after," Jason said. "And that's why I wanted to get out of there as quickly as I could. I mean, I watched it happen my whole life. Memorial Day rolls around, the tourists start coming in, money starts flowing. Since they're spending the money, some of them think that gives the free reign to act however they want. And that the people who work at the fried seafood places and ice cream shops and bike and boat rental stores, all these people are just supposed to take it. You wouldn't believe the way some of the tourists acted. I mean, most of them were fine, just trying to enjoy their vacation. And I wouldn't want to take that from them. But you could always count on there being a handful of people who were just completely insufferable. Who would expect you to do every last thing they wanted, no matter how ridiculous or completely unreasonable it was. I couldn't do it. I knew I couldn't, even when I was just a kid. All through school I worked during the offseason as a bike mechanic at the local shop. And every summer, I'd quit the bike shop job because I couldn't deal with the tourists. I'd make sure I'd saved enough to be able to get by, and sometimes I'd help out with odd jobs—you know, home repairs and stuff, for local folks. And then, once Labor Day passed and all the tourists went away, I'd go back to the bike shop and my boss would re-hire me. I did that all through high school."

I took a sip of my coffee. "So you had the whole summer off? Doesn't sound too bad."

"Oh, it wasn't. I mean, everyone thought I was crazy

working 30 hours a week and going to school, but they certainly weren't saying the same thing when summer rolled around and I was sleeping in and not having to deal with all the crap they were. I guess that experience really showed me that if you want—or don't want—to do something, you're going to find a way that works for you." He sighed. "Or at least, that's how I used to think of it working out. Now, I'm not so sure."

"Oh yeah?" I said. "Why's that?"

He shrugged. "You know, life, I guess. When I moved out here, I had some pretty specific ideas for how I wanted my life to turn out. I remember loading up the car and driving out here from Maine, how the possibilities seemed as endless as the stretch of highway in front of me. Just the anticipation of it was thrilling—the not knowing, but imagining how great it was going to turn out. It didn't all have to go exactly according to plan, but there were certain things I wanted to do, and, more importantly, certain things I *didn't* want to do, which, I hate to say, I happen to be doing."

"Like what?"

"Like...working Monday through Friday, eight to five, in some stuffy office. Although it does have a decent view of the ocean. Which is kind of like this terrible temptation, it's like taunting you, like, *Look where you could be if you weren't here at your job.*" He laughed and waved his hand dismissively. "But never mind that stuff, man. I don't want to inundate you with my sob story while you're just trying to enjoy your cup of coffee. I should just be thankful I have a job, right? And I am. I am." The look on his face, though, suggested he felt otherwise.

"Talk about it all you want," I told him. "I was actually in a pretty similar situation that you were when I first got out here. The company I worked for, actually, let me transfer out here and from there I was able to get out on my own, which has been really great. But I was stuck for a while, too. So I know where you're coming from."

"Yeah?" He smiled. "That's actually really great to hear. It helps sometimes to know that you're not the only one. I just sometimes can't believe that this is where I am in life. I feel like I was so determined not to have this kind of working life when I was a kid—when you don't even have to be working—and now here I am, doing exactly what I didn't want to be doing."

"What is it you'd rather be doing?"

"You know," he said, tracing his finger along the lid of his coffee cup, "at one point I thought I knew, but it's been so long that I've even let myself think about it that I don't know. I have no idea, and I think that's the part that scares me the most."

Jason and I talked for a few more minutes before he had to go back to work. Before we parted ways, we exchanged phone numbers. I could tell that our brief conversation had reignited something. It had awakened his inner lion, which may have been hibernating all those years.

IT IS INTERESTING to realize that at some point in our lives, usually once we're out of childhood, we stop saying "play" and we start saying work," and we stop saying" game" and start using "job" instead.

Work and play are usually considered mutually exclusive. The two don't go hand-in-hand, except for the very, very lucky. We think, *Well, not everyone can make a living being a painter, or an athlete, or a writer, or a supermodel. Not everyone is so fortunate to get paid enough to survive doing something they love.* The problem with this way of thinking is that many people don't actually realize what their gift is. They believe that others around them might have a gift, but they themselves do not. There is an audience for everything, especially in this day and age. And there is no better feeling than realizing that something you truly enjoy doing can be turned into a profitable business, a way for you to make your living.

There will be obstacles, of course, perhaps even starting with your own belief systems. You might feel a range of contrasting emotions, simultaneously pulled in two different directions. So which one is the right way?

Most likely, one part of you is saying that you should be realistic, you should play it safe. Your job might not be your most favorite thing in the whole world, but it's a regular paycheck, you get great benefits, and by the time you're 65, you'll be drawing on that pension or 401(k). These are valid reasons. These are realistic reasons, rooted in stability. What these reasons generally don't take into account is the day-to-day. Do you want to spend nine hours a day, five or six days a week, in a cubicle, doing someone else's work? It can be both liberating and infuriating when you first start to realize how much your cubicle is actually like a cage, and you, and your inner lion, are locked in. Now that you have realized this, you can begin taking the steps to get out of the cubicle—to take everything you've learned and experienced and move onward, toward something else.

BUT WHAT IF you feel like you're up against a lot when you decide it's time to start taking the steps to get out of the cubicle? Your family, spouse, friends, neighbors—they might not understand. They might flat out disagree with you. You yourself might have feeling that are holding you back: *What about the mortgage, the kids' college fund, the credit card bills, the car payments…?* The list goes on and on (longer for some than others). But for the great majority of people, there will always be *something* on that list. When you're struggling with something and right in the thick of it, it's easy to think that others have it easier, or have more advantages than you do. This type of thinking is untrue and is really only going to be detrimental to yourself. You are not the only one with these hurdles. This is not to minimize the things in life that you are dealing with, but some people almost seem to enjoy thinking that they're special in a bad way. Instead of using your children, or your house payments, or anything else, as your ticket to why you're not doing something, use it as your ticket to do exactly that.

Maybe you've put off doing what you really want to be doing because there's something in front of you that is preventing you from moving forward. You think, *Once*

I get this taken care of, then *I can proceed with doing what I want.* Yet so often, you take care of that first problem only to find that there's one right behind it. And another behind that. And so on and so on. Of course it is tempting to want to wait until the moment is perfect. *If I can just get to that point,* you think, *then things will go smoothly; it will all work out.* It's very easy to get trapped in this way of thinking and lay the blame of your inaction on the external things, but I cannot stress to you enough that there will always be something that will be in the way. And if you continually tell yourself that you'll get started once the dog has gone to the vet, or the leak in the roof is fixed, or the transmission on the car is replaced, you're going to always find yourself in the role of the victim. A victim is someone who has had something done to him or her. Many people are victims of their own lives, without even realizing it. It's a very easy trap to fall into, and once there, it can be difficult to get out of.

As on any journey, transitions will have to be made. Whether you're going from the cubicle to your own business or the grocery store parking lot back to your house, some sort of transition will be taking place. Clearly, making the journey from the grocery store parking lot back home should be fraught with a lot less stress and anxiety than going from the cubicle out on your own, unless, say, you're living in Los Angeles and trying to take the southbound 405 on a Friday afternoon. Really, though, transitioning can be difficult. Even if it's something that you've wanted to do for a long time, it can still be scary.

Be aware of where you land in a transition. Maybe you are now ready to leave the cubicle and start the business you've always wanted to. And maybe in order to do so, you need to downgrade certain aspects of your life. This might not feel like forward progress.

If your cubicle job provided you with paid time off and a decent benefits package, striking out on your own could require you to forego sick days and a two-week vacation, at least at first. While you might not have been fulfilled at your job in the cubicle, you were probably comfortable, in terms of knowing where your next paycheck was coming from and having certain perks that are usually not feasible in the first year or two of starting your own business. *Well, that kind of sucks,* you might find yourself thinking. Most people would agree that having paid time off and a comprehensive healthcare package are very nice things. And they are, but what are you giving up in order to have those? Getting out of the cubicle will allow you a freedom that is impossible to obtain in a corporate job.

By definition, a transition means a change. A transition is a movement, or a series of movements, from one thing to the next. You have point A; you have point B. The space in between the two is your transition. It might not be a straight shot from one to the other. It might zigzag; it might romp to and fro; it might make a couple pit stops along the way. It is not your destination, but the route you take in order to get there. Yet sometimes, people will find themselves stuck in the transition. What was supposed to be a temporary situation has suddenly become static; five years have passed and you suddenly realize you are still in this "transitional" phase. Being aware of the fact that you are transitioning can help keep you from getting stuck. You do not have to expect things to happen overnight, but know that you are constantly moving toward your goal, and keep momentum on your side.

Chapter 7

The Layers of an Onion

A lot of times, parents and other adults in our lives think they're helping us by ingraining the idea that you need to find a good job in order to have a roof over your head and food in the refrigerator and your other basic needs met. Anything else we happen to get in the process is just extra; it's a bonus—something we should be thankful for but not come to expect. This is the Hy-Vee mindset in action. As we go through school, this way of thinking is reinforced: Our teachers assign us tasks and we are given responsibilities we must uphold, in the form of homework. Whether or not we find this homework stimulating is of little concern. We do it because we're supposed to—because everyone else is. We are expected to follow instructions, do as we're told, and not buck the system. In mainstream, public schools, intuition is not something that is generally talked about; there is no class geared at knowing when to pay attention to the goose bumps you get about a certain idea. These things are not nurtured, and in worst-case scenarios they're suppressed or stamped out. It's maddening, if you stop and think about it. We are at our best when we're able to pursue that which interests us, so why on earth are we continually taught that we must put other things ahead of that which we truly love?

Really, it is vital that we be able to recognize those moments when we get chills—when something has piqued our interest in a noticeable way. It might be goose bumps or a shiver down your spine. It could be a quiet, persistent nagging—the feeling that you're not doing something you should be, even if you're not exactly sure yet what that something is. Try not to ignore these feelings. They can be very easy to dismiss, especially amid the busy-ness of everyday life, but if you practice being in tune with the present moment, more often than not, you will find yourself noticing these chills—this feeling of your passion starting to come alive.

This is one of the things Jason and I spent a lot of time talking about when we first started hanging out. As we move into adulthood, unless we're extremely talented at something, it's all too easy to put your passion on the back burner, to dismiss it as something that you are really only able to do when you have the time, or the energy, or the resources. Things that you were wild about as a child are often left back in childhood, with so much other good stuff. This is exactly what happened with Jason. He moved to San Diego and met a girl, and five years ago, their son was born. This was both an exciting and incredibly stressful time for Jason, as it is for most people who are experiencing parenthood for the first time. For a while, Jason was grateful he had a steady paycheck and a job that provided him and his family with health insurance and allowed him to take some paid time off each year.

But lately he'd been feeling the stirrings of discontent, yet he didn't know what to do about it. This is another very common scenario people find themselves in: unhappy, but unsure of what to do. Identifying this unhappiness is an important step, because only then will you be able to come up with ideas and solutions to get yourself out of this chronic unhappiness.

"So, what's your passion?" I asked Jason one day. "If money were no factor, what's the one thing you could see yourself doing? That you'd *want* to be doing?"

"Bicycles," he said instantly. There was not a moment's hesitation. *A-ha*, I thought. *There is his answer right there. And he didn't even have to think about it.*

"Do something with that."

"Yeah, sure," he said, smiling wryly. "As if it were that easy. I can just see the thrilled expression on Stephanie's face if I told her I quit my job and decided to open my own bike shop."

"Did you ever think," I asked, "that maybe if you stopped looking at the situation as something impossible, or something that your loved ones are going to hate you for doing, that maybe you might see it differently?"

He considered this for a moment. "I guess I never thought of it that way," he said. "It's not that I want to think I'm stuck here with no other options; I'm just so bogged down with bills and work and everyday life that taking anything else on seems like it would be utterly impossible."

"But maybe it's not."

"Maybe it's not," he agreed. "I'd like to think that's true."

"Can you get from liking to think that it's true to *actually* believing that it's true?"

"It seems like it might be a leap. But maybe I could. Sitting here with you, I kind of feel a little removed from the situation, and that's sort of allowing me to see that maybe it's not impossible. It's just so easy when you're rushing to work or trying to make a budget for the next two months, to think that you could not possibly fit anything else into your life, *especially* if it has something to do with, you know, passion."

"Well, we certainly wouldn't want that," I said jokingly. "But really, though. Bikes are your passion. That's great. Now, examine that a little further. How would you turn that into something that you could also make a living at?"

"Oh, I've got tons of ideas," he said. "I used to think about this all the time when I was younger. I mean, back then it was mostly just daydream sort of stuff, like *This is what I'd do if I ever won the lottery* sort of thing. I'd love to have a shop that's kind of like a collective. You know, people can come in, learn mechanics, work on their bikes. Foster a real sense of community, you know? And fat bikes—I've really gotten into those."

"Fat bikes?"

"Picture a mountain bike, except the tires and rims are about three times as wide. Great for riding in loose sand, snow, that sort of thing. This past weekend, actually, I just took a ride from Torrey Pines down to La Jolla and it was awesome."

"That sounds like fun."

"It is; we'll have to go some time. One of my favorite things to do is cruise down the beach. You can get to some really awesome places that you might not be able to if you were on foot. Not too many people know about fat bikes yet, though, and I'd love to be able to help facilitate that sort of thing. It's so much fun."

That next weekend was a holiday weekend. Jason had Monday off, so we took two fat bikes out for a ride down the beach. And wouldn't you know, it really was just as much fun as he'd led me to believe.

IT WAS EASY, in talking with Jason, to see how passionate he was about bikes. As an outside observer of Jason's situation, it was clear to me that he should be doing something with bikes, not sitting in a cubicle for nine hours a day. Just seeing him talk about building bicycles, or going for a ride and discovering a new trail, or taking the fat bikes out on the beach at low tide, it was easy to tell that bikes were his passion. They were what gave him chills and got him excited. The expression on his face changed, his eyes lit up. His energy shifted—became more vibrant and electric. It was tangible, almost. We all have something that does that for us, although it can be easy to forget. But what is it that sends a shiver up and down your spine? What makes you smile, in spite of yourself? These are all signs, clues, if you need help remembering. Pay attention to the next time you find your mind wandering, and consider what it is you're thinking about. I bet, more often than not, that when Jason's daydreaming at work, it's about bikes. If you find that you're one of the people who dismisses these notions, don't be too hard on yourself. Most likely, you've been told things are a certain way for years and years, and it's going to take time to unlearn some of these beliefs and ways of thinking. There is an art of unlearning, and in order to program new things with you, you have to unlearn much of what you've probably come to believe as the truth. This is no easy undertaking, and you shouldn't expect to have mastered it in a night. Just as you wouldn't dream of getting on a horse for the first time and being able to take it over a 5-foot-high jump, so it is with breaking out of old thought patterns.

Liken your journey out of the cubicle to peeling away the layers of an onion. One of the very first layers you're going to peel away and examine is your belief about money. What do you want money for? Have you ever really asked yourself that question? Maybe not, because all along we're taught that we need to get a job in order to make money to provide x, y, and z. So maybe upon first asking yourself that question, your automatic response is: *to pay the mortgage. For my children's college education. To put an addition on the house. To go on vacation.* Or any number of other things.

Beyond their basic needs being met, some people might have a hard time articulating what else they might like money for. Perhaps they do have a great business idea they'd like to pursue, but fear that, in the current situation, it would be impractical, or foolish. That is just another layer of the onion to pull back and examine. And also be aware that, though it is not something that can be seen, the law of attraction can and will play a large role in the way your life turns out. Believing that you must stay in the cubicle could very likely prevent situations from occurring that could help you get *out* of the cubicle. If you believe that things are generally bad and there is nothing you can do about them, those are the sorts of energies and influences that will impact your life. If you believe you are stuck and there is no way to get out, with no solutions other than to stick out the situation you're already in, you will remain there until you manage to change the way you look at things.

THE REASON IT is vitally important to peel back these onion layers and examine your beliefs is that once you are out of the cubicle and going after things you are interested in, you need to make sure what you are pursuing is in alignment with your beliefs. Some people are so thrilled to find themselves no longer in the cubicle that they jump headfirst into the first project that comes their way. Enthusiasm is crucial, but you have to be wise with where you put your energies. This is why sometimes people find themselves pouring their entire being into a business or a project yet not seeing results. They feel like they are working so hard yet achieving so little—a frustrating experience for anyone. Generally, this sort of thing happens when what is being pursued is not in alignment with your beliefs. It's like tuning into a radio station except you're two points off. You'll still be able to hear the music, but there's going to be a lot of static and the signal will fade in and out. It's going to be difficult to hear and it's not going to be a pleasant experience. Aligning your actions with your beliefs harmonizes your energetic vibrational levels and is like changing the dial those two points so the music can come in crystal clear.

Finding this alignment is not always the easiest thing to do, and it often requires us to examine thoughts and beliefs that we might rather ignore. But ignoring these beliefs will only perpetuate a cycle, and if you are trying to break free of a certain way of thinking or a certain way of life, staying in a cycle is going to be detrimental in the end.

In college, I became friendly with a girl named Lauren. She was a sweet girl who was motivated and talented, and always put other people ahead of herself. It was just her way. She was the sort of girl that people just enjoyed being around—the type of person who made everyone feel special. For almost our entire junior year, she was involved with a guy who didn't treat her very well. It was perplexing and disturbing; how could such a nice person end up in that sort of relationship? I wasn't the only one of Lauren's friends who was concerned about her relationship with this guy, but for a long time, she just brushed off anything we had to say about it. It was difficult to watch, but we could only hope that eventually, she'd realize that she deserved to be treated with more respect.

Well, the day finally came when she ended it with that guy, and I can tell you, her friends and family were all quite relieved. *Good!* we all thought. *Now she can get involved with someone who will treat her right.* The relief was short-lived though, because a few months later Lauren started seeing someone who actually made the other guy look good in comparison.

Now, you could say that Lauren just had bad luck with guys. But I think if you stop and peel back some of the layers and really examine them, you might find a more substantial answer. Perhaps Lauren thought she deserved to be treated like that. Maybe many of the adult relationships she saw growing up were dysfunctional and she came to believe that as normal. Even though she had numerous people telling her that her relationship was unhealthy and that she deserved something better, she wasn't able to manifest that. Lauren's situation is not an uncommon one, unfortunately. In order for Lauren to find a healthy, mutually beneficial relationship, she's going to have to unlearn many of the beliefs she previously held about how someone's partner is supposed to treat them. Unlearning long-held beliefs can be a painful process. Some of these beliefs might be deeply ingrained in you, so much so that you don't even realize it. In Lauren's case, I believe she was operating on a subconscious level when it came to the type of men she was attracted to and found herself with.

Maybe your relationship with your current job is an unhealthy one. Maybe your job is like a partner who doesn't know how to treat you well, or who continually takes but does not give back. And maybe you believe, deep down, that this is the way it should be, even though you don't wake up in the morning excited to go to work, and by the end of the work week you're exhausted and eager for two days off to recharge and hopefully have enough of a break that you've got it in yourself to face the new work week. If this is so, make the commitment to yourself to examine where these feelings are coming from. Don't be afraid to pull back the layers, one by one. You might be surprised at what you find.

Chapter 8

Currency

So many of our decisions and life choices are based around money, whether directly or indirectly. We live in a society where this is necessary, and where having enough money is seen not just as a privilege but as a right, if you are willing to put in the hard work. Because money permeates so much of our lives, it is worth it to give careful consideration to your views on it, how you handle it, and what you hope your money can do for you.

Currency is derived from the root word *current,* which is a synonym for *flow.* I think it's a good way to think of money, because the bottom line is, for it to function as it should, it needs to have a certain flow. This means give and receive, receive and give. It is a fine line, though, and the learning curve is steeper for some than others. In a materialistic culture such as ours, it can be very easy to get caught up in having the latest and greatest car, computer, television, stereo system, et cetera. Credit card companies start stalking you with too-good-to-be-true offers before you're even old enough to vote and buying things when you don't actually have the funds to pay for them isn't the type of flow you want from your money, either.

So, your relationship to money is about finding balance. How are you going to generate enough money to provide the things you both want and need? First, you need to figure out what those things are. Don't be afraid to ask yourself these questions. Much like "play" became "work" as we outgrew our childhoods, our sense of wonder and curiosity about the world around us has also diminished. Children are known—sometimes notoriously so—for asking questions. *Why is that like this? How does this work? Where did that come from?* Yet as we age, the questions become fewer and fewer. Perhaps it's because we're older and we think we know more. Or maybe there just isn't enough time in the day to wonder about anything other than what is immediately affecting us.

But curiosity and questioning things are great ways to help yourself discover what it is you want to do outside of the cubicle. Perhaps you already have some idea, but asking yourself these questions—the whys, the hows—is going to help you clarify your ideas. Because remember: The energy that you're putting into a new business is not just your time or money; it is the overall commitment to yourself and your passion. That is real flow, real current. Adding those extra layers and extra details can really heighten the level of commitment you're giving yourself and your new business.

Try putting an hourly rate on your life. Say that's $50 an hour, or do $100, if you'd like a nice, round number.

Use whatever amount you want, though, really. Now, apply that hourly rate to your life. Are there things in your life that you could actually be saving money on by having other people do? The old saying is definitely true, and your time is money. Many people spend much of their time doing things they either don't want to do or aren't any good at. Depending on your current financial situation, it might make more sense to pay someone to do the things you either are no good at or don't have any interest in doing.

Some people might balk at the idea of this. It might sound unsavory, or like something only the ultra-privileged get to do. But if you think about it, you're probably already doing it, to some degree. Many people take their cars in to get the oil changed. If you're not interested in the inner workings of your automobile, or weren't taught how to do so, it's worth it to pay the $30 to have it done by someone who already knows how to do it. You'd probably be likely to pay someone to have the carpets cleaned. Sure, you're certainly *capable* of doing it yourself, but it would require a lot of time and effort on your part when it could be spent better elsewhere. Or how about getting a haircut? Again, that's another activity you could do yourself but probably don't. It just makes sense to have someone, with experience, do it. Look at other areas of your life and see where there are things that could fall in this category. Paying someone to do something that you don't enjoy or are not good at is not shirking your responsibilities. It is a way of time and money management that can be greatly beneficial, as you will then have the chance to focus your energy in areas that are of interest to you as you work toward moving out of the cubicle.

If you have the end outcome in mind, that's great. If you don't, that's okay, too. Believing that you need to know exactly what your next move is before you can continue is often limiting and can prevent you from taking the next crucial step. This is not to say that you shouldn't have plans or try to envision how things might work out in the future, but do not let that hold you back if you don't have everything worked out exactly. It is all too easy to never actually get started because you might not have a clear picture of all the steps you plan to take. This requires trust—trust in the universe, in the process, and, most of all, in yourself. The first step is often the hardest, but if you don't want to stay in a holding pattern of never doing, then you've got to find it in yourself to make the move. Once you get going, you will find that it's easier to keep the momentum and that the universe will help you along the way by opening doors you might not have been able to anticipate.

I like to think of this as someone reading a map but only being able to see a certain distance around them all the time. Or, more recently, I went for a nighttime mountain bike ride with Jason, which was scary and exhilarating and a whole different experience. He knew the trails; I didn't. I had a decent head lamp attached to my helmet, bright enough to light the way about 6 feet in front of me. This might sound adequate, but the first time I tried night riding, I was certain I was in way over my head and would probably not make it off the trail in one piece. Aside from the cone of light illuminating the 6 feet in front of me, I was surrounded by darkness. At first I rode slowly, with much trepidation. Who knew what sorts of things were out there that I couldn't yet see! I could get sideswiped by any number of things and knocked onto my ass. It didn't happen, but that nighttime bike ride is a good metaphor for your journey out of the cubicle. You've got to put some degree of faith in the fact that, though you can't know exactly where you'll be in a year, or five years, putting trust in yourself and the universe will get you to where you need to be. And that night, out on the trail, once I put that trust in myself, I was able to cruise along and have a really wonderful time. And I made it home safely and eager to go out and try it again.

Chapter 9

The Energetic Enema

A friend came up with an interesting phrase. We were talking with someone who was just starting to come to the realization that he wasn't doing what he wanted to with his life but didn't know how to take the first steps to change it. He was so used to the way things were he could only imagine a different sort of life for himself, but not actually make a move to manifest those desires in reality.

"What you need," my friend told him, "is an energetic enema."

This elicited laughter from those within earshot, and I don't know how seriously anyone that day took the phrase, but it does a very good job describing exactly what you might need if you're finding it difficult to get started on a new direction.

This is similar, in a way, to exercise. It's somewhat of a paradox that you might be feeling exhausted and rather crummy, yet if you can motivate yourself to get out for a run or a bike ride or even a nice walk, you'll feel better. You'll feel more awake and enlivened, and generally be in better spirits. So how did you somehow gain *more* energy by expending energy? You used up the stagnant, tired energy that had been circulating, freeing up room for new, positive energy. The same is true for thoughts and ideas. Cleaning yourself out of the same old thought patterns makes room for new ideas and lets your mind go in directions it might not have been previously able to. And there are many ways to do this. Some people find it beneficial to go on a weekend retreat, a respite away from their daily life. Granted, this isn't a possibility for everyone, and if you're one of those people, you may find yourself wondering how you can cleanse yourself from old thought patterns.

You might not be familiar with something called the Milton Model Language Patterns, but you've probably heard the term *hypnosis* before. The Milton Model Language Patterns were named after American psychiatrist Milton Erickson, who specialized in helping his patients by use of hypnosis. From Milton Erickson's work, Richard Bandler and John Grinder created neuro-linguistic programming, or NLP. Under hypnosis, you are far more receptive to suggestibility. Basically, when you are under hypnosis, the subconscious mind comes to the forefront while the conscious part takes a back seat. You may not be aware of it, but your subconscious mind is always hard at work. The subconscious mind is responsible for the dreams you have when you sleep, and though these dreams often don't make sense to our conscious mind, they are our subconscious mind's way of figuring things out.

WHEN IT COMES to energy and starting on your project—any project—the first step is to always be in front of your creative project. That literally means the universe is not going to open the door for you if it doesn't think you could open that door yourself. If you're waiting for something to happen before you take the step, then that something is waiting for you. Waiting for the perfect opportunity to start your business or to undertake a new creative project means you will never begin, because the perfect time does not exist. There will always be something happening that will give you pause—that will make you say, *Well, once* that *is resolved, then I'll be able to get started.* And perhaps that thing does get resolved, only for something else to come up that you feel you need to take care of first. And so it goes.

It's a lot like having a baby. Babies gestate for a finite period: nine months and they're done. Most expectant parents will openly admit that they're not ready for their child's impending arrival, but what choice do they have? Ready or not, it's going to happen. So don't wait for everything to align perfectly to get started on your projects; begin doing what you can now. Remind yourself that there will never be the "perfect" time, because that concept does not actually exist. And it's okay if you don't know what the end is going to look like. Because you know what? Even if you do have a very concrete idea in your mind of what you'd like the final outcome to be, there's a good chance it will look nothing like that when you finally get there, anyway. This is not to say that if you *do* have an end goal you're not going to achieve it, but things will come up along the way that might change what your final outcome ultimately looks like. What you need to remember is that in order for *anything* to happen, you need to get started.

And one way to do this, especially if you're feeling some trepidation about getting started, is to broaden your scope enough, to chunk up enough, to let things start moving even just a little bit, because once it's moving, it will keep moving. And this is how projects take on a life of their own.

Chunking up and *chunking down* are two NLP terms. In chunking up, you broaden the scope of an idea or topic. Essentially, you can go as broad as the universe or beyond. For example: A car is a mode of transportation. Transportation is a type of movement. Movement is something that pretty much everything does, whether it's you getting to work or the tides or the planets orbiting around the sun. To chunk back down, you go in the opposite direction. Using our example of transportation again, instead of cars, let's choose airplanes, another type of transportation. A Boeing 737 is a specific—and most popular—type of passenger airplane. Virgin America is an airline that uses 737s. You can chunk down even more and say, "first class seats in that type of plane" or "the specific types of peanuts they have on that flight." And from there: "the salt on those peanuts."

Chunking up gives you a broad scope of whatever it is you want to examine. By getting more vague and abstract, you are able to encompass a broader spectrum. Conversely, chunking down requires you to get specific. As you chunk down, you can go multiple directions. Perhaps instead of cars or airplanes, you want choose farm machinery, or horse and buggies, or dogsleds. This process is known as *chunking laterally*.

Using these techniques are helpful in a whole slew of things, including communication, negotiation skills, problem solving, interpersonal relationships. It can also be useful as you move from the cubicle toward the life that you really want. If, perhaps, you don't know exactly what that life looks like, chunk up until you've gone broad enough that something resonates. Once you get comfortable here, you can begin chunking down. If, at any point, you start chunking down and an idea doesn't sit well with you, all you need to do is chunk back up and then go a different direction.

Use these techniques to help you determine exactly what it is you want to be doing. I know you're thinking about how wonderful it would be to own your own company, or to have the freedom to start that creative project you've had on the back burner for so long now. You might be at the point right now where you feel like you haven't made much progress, but it's good you're even thinking about the direction you want to go in. It is good that you're taking the steps needed to get out of the cubicle, and the fact that you're reading this book means you're already one step closer to being on your own and working for yourself.

IT CAN ALSO help to remind yourself of the characteristics of a lion. You can even ask: *What would a lion do?* Remember: Lions are powerful but can also go with the flow. Don't be afraid to raise your standards of where the middle is. Sometimes people are afraid to live too high because thy fear the fall, whether or not this fall would actually happen. They think, *If I'm happy now, I'm going to have to come down at some point.* And that leaves the mind free to conjure up all sorts of nightmarish scenarios, which makes staying stagnant, staying in a safe zone, all the more appealing.

Chapter 10

Alignment

Now that you've seen how I managed to get out of the cubicle, I'd like to talk about things you can do to help facilitate the process for yourself. Jason was able to apply many of these things to his own life, and that he and I were both able to do it means that anyone can. We're not superheroes; we're not business gurus. The fact that you are reading this book means that you are already thinking about these sorts of things. You have already taken that first step, and now moving forward will only get easier. So perhaps you didn't even realize that you were getting the ball rolling, so to speak, yet you have and you should acknowledge that as a small victory for yourself. Each small win is something to be proud of. Good work.

FAMILIARIZING YOURSELF WITH the law of inertia can help all aspects of your life. An object in motion will stay in motion. This applies to ideas as well. Ideas will spawn new ideas, activity will breed activity. So if you've been stagnant in your job for a while, it might initially seem like an impossible task to anything than what you've been doing now. Start slow. Don't expect things to change overnight, but you've got to take the first small step. And that tiny bit is like the first handfuls of snow, packed tight and small, that will eventually form a large snowball, if you put in enough effort and gain enough momentum.

After Jason had let the idea of opening his own bike shop percolate for a little while, he started networking with people who might be able to help him or otherwise inspire him. As you're considering what it is you'd like to do and how you might go about doing it, consider who you might be able to reach out to. You might feel nervous at first, or think that people are going to be skeptical about your plans. *You want to do* what?! You can already hear their laughter in your head. But that's just an old thought pattern, trying to keep you in check and trying to keep you in your safe zone, which might be comfortable but isn't where you want to be.

I have found myself feeling incredibly lost at times when I'm between creative projects. So much so that it can be almost paralyzing, and even though I've been in this situation before and gotten out of it, for a few scary moments, I always think that this time I'm not going to be able to get myself out of it—this time, I'm done for.

You may have found yourself in a similar scenario. One of the best things to do at a time like this is to go broad. Refer back to the previous chapter if you need to, but you are basically going to chunk up until you get to somewhere that feels comfortable. Imagine a train, if you will. When you're in the middle of a project, you're on the train, and if things are going well, that train is hurtling along the tracks, so fast that it's like a blur against the landscape.

But when you're between projects, when you're not sure what to do next, it can feel like you're suddenly off the train, standing by the side, wanting to jump on but not knowing the first way to go about doing it. What if you try to jump on and miss? What if you get hurt? Such questions can render you unable to do anything at all, except stand there and watch the rushing train go by. Now imagine chunking up—going broad. This is going to slow the train down. The broader you go, the slower the train will get, until it's slowed enough that you feel comfortable to get back on. At this point in time, you might decide you want to just get your bearings and not speed things up too much. Or you might find yourself full of new ideas. Chunk down—get more specific. The more specific you get, the faster the train will go, but you're back on it now, momentum is on your side, and now, all of a sudden, you're no longer between projects but right there in the middle of a new one.

REGARDLESS OF HOW much momentum you have, though, if your alignment is out of whack, you're going to run into unnecessary challenges. When your conscious and subconscious are out of line, there will be discordance. It might be subtle, and you might not even realize it. How then, if it's so hard to detect, are you going to know if your conscious and subconscious mind are out of alignment? Often, you will notice an energetic shift, a feeling of discomfort or unease. Perhaps your conscious mind is telling you that you really want something, yet your subconscious is adamant that you don't. When we are aligned, our internal and external will be a mirror, reflecting the same back. Very often, though, people's desires are out of sync. There are many reasons for this. You might have a great idea for a business, or a project that you're very eager to undertake. Yet perhaps your subconscious is telling you that it's not a good idea, that your idea is going to fail, that people are going to make fun of you or somehow think less of you if you go forward with it. Or maybe you find yourself continually striving for things you don't actually want. Your subconscious is totally fine with what you have and the way you are doing things, yet your conscious mind is constantly ridiculing you, making comparisons to your neighbors or your co-workers, and admonishing you to keep up with the Joneses, even if deep inside, that sort of thing doesn't really matter to you.

The subconscious mind is a very powerful thing that most people don't give much thought to or spend time trying to understand. The subconscious mind controls the autonomic nervous system, which includes things like heartbeat, breathing, and digestion. These very important functions take place without you thinking about them. Suppressed memories also exist in the subconscious mind, perhaps coming to light through dreams or in hypnosis. Your subconscious mind, in fact, retains everything that you have ever learned or experienced. Yet it is your conscious mind that filters what it deems necessary to remember, and everything else is pushed back to the subconscious.

How, then, do you access these thoughts and these memories? What sorts of things can you do to bring your conscious mind and your subconscious into alignment?

Both hypnosis and NLP override the conscious mind in order to get to the subconscious. By getting to the subconscious mind, you can go back to whatever thought, feeling, or belief you had that is now causing you to be out of alignment. This sort of regression work allows you to re-process the event in a more beneficial manner.

Another way to help you access your subconscious thoughts is through what is known as "stream of consciousness" writing. This basically means you give yourself permission to write down whatever thoughts come to your mind, regardless of how zany or illogical they might seem. Most of us will find that we're harnessed by the internal editor, that voice saying that we're not using correct grammar or we spelled a word incorrectly or that thought we just wrote down is invalid or nonsense or just doesn't make sense. It can take some time to get past the internal editor, but just plow ahead. It will get easier over time. If you have fear or anxiety about getting out of the cubicle, write it down. Don't stop to review what you've written; just let the thoughts flow and write or type them as they come. Eventually, you will notice that the internal editor has quieted, that the conscious mind has stepped aside and you are writing now from a deeper place. Things are coming up that you're getting down on the paper that you hadn't even thought about, or realized that you were feeling anxious over. And just seeing them there, on the page or on the screen, helps.

Visualization is another tool that you will find very helpful when it comes to alignment and manifesting your goals. This technique goes hand-in-hand with positive thinking and, together, the two can be very powerful. Creative visualization is like watching a scene from a movie play out in your head, except you're the director. You're also the set designer, the production and casting crew, and probably the star of the show. Allow yourself to imagine exactly what it is you want. This is when having an end goal in mind can be helpful, but again, if you don't, that doesn't mean you can't benefit from creative visualization. Let yourself really see whatever it is you're working on or would like to be working on. Perhaps your goal is to be out of the cubicle in a year's time, doing freelance work instead. Imagine yourself, then, a year from now, and instead of a commute into the office, you now just walk down the hallway to your home office. See yourself sitting at your desk, working on projects where you have set the deadline. Let yourself experience what you imagine it feels like to be your own boss. Because this is your visualization—your movie—

let yourself experience it as if it is already true. Repeat these visualizations as often as you want.

Positive thinking is like a less-intensive form of creative visualization. If creative visualization can be likened to watching a movie, positive thinking might be like reading a book. Because in this case, all you need are words. Something short and simple can be very effective. It can be as vague or specific as you'd like. It might be *I am a good person.* or *I have the skills necessary to run my own business.*

Jason started keeping a journal, just a little spiral-bound notebook that he could carry in his back pocket. He used this to write down positive thoughts—things that he could look over to keep him inspired and motivated. The journal was also a helpful space for him to work out obstacles and challenges that came up. One of the first things he started off with was writing down what he didn't like about his current job. You might have a similar list. He went through this list and then contrasted that list with things that would make his working life enjoyable. In this way, he was able to turn his negative feelings toward his job to positive ones that he'd be able to work toward.

Keep in mind, though, that positive thinking does not mean you have to sugarcoat everything. Ignoring or glossing over problems or issues that come up is not going to help you in the long run and is only going to hinder you from staying in alignment.

Be prepared to encounter people who might try to give you a hard time about what you're trying to do. You might have some very big ideas—some great ideas that others just might not seem capable of understanding. They might rag on you for giving up your good-paying job, or tell you horror stories about how a friend of a friend of a friend tried to start a business that failed and they went bankrupt and had to move back into their parents' basement. Try to take such comments in stride and realize that, more likely than not, the person is saying them out of fear, or jealousy, or perhaps just concern that you're not doing the right thing. If you are in alignment with what you're doing, nothing that anyone else says is going to deter you from your course.

One of the biggest difficulties Jason ran into on his way out of the cubicle was the doubts his spouse and family had. This is understandable. His wife was afraid that he was taking too big of a chance that could backfire and leave them with nothing. He had a family to consider, after all, and couldn't just throw everything away to pursue what she thought was a boyhood passion. It's very possible that you might find yourself in a similar position and have to defend your choices and actions to those you consider closest. I'm not going to tell you that this won't be difficult, but when your conscious and subconscious are in alignment, things will be more streamlined. This isn't to say there won't be any struggles or difficulties to overcome; there very well may be plenty of those, but you will feel better equipped to handle them. It is, in a way, like the runner's high, where everything seems to be operating seamlessly. What you're doing might still be challenging, but when you are in alignment, a natural cohesion exists that makes it easier to overcome whatever problems you might be faced with.

Chapter 11

Upgrade

We live in a vibrational world. This can be a difficult concept for some people to accept, because vibrations are not things that can be seen. But they are there, nonetheless. The term *subtle body* refers to the non-physical components that make up all living things. Essentially, energy. Things happen in the world where we are at a higher vibrational level. And you can do things to keep yourself at this higher level. It can be something as simple as eating certain foods. Eating foods that are minimally processed, organic, and as close to their natural form as possible, will keep harmful toxins and pesticides from your body. Become aware of your thoughts. If you've never really tuned in to all the thoughts that go through your mind on any given day, you might really be surprised how much chatter is going on in there!

Pay special attention to any thoughts that are negative or seem overly critical. Much has been written on the benefits of positive thinking, and if you are unfamiliar with this practice, it is worth checking out. And if positive thoughts can impact your life, you better believe that the negative ones can, too. If you are not accustomed to paying attention to your thoughts, or turning negative ones into positive ones, it may take some time before you get the hang of it.

The people you choose to surround yourself with can also affect your vibrational level. I think we've all had the experience of being around someone from whom we just didn't get a good feeling. Or have you ever been hanging out with someone, and after you leave, you feel like they've drained all the energy from you? You might not have even been doing anything that exerting, yet there you are, feeling completely wiped out. Maybe you've just brushed it off, dismissed it as you not drinking enough coffee that morning or being overtired for some reason or another, but if you really stop to think about it, you might come to the realization that your energy, your *subtle body*, is affected by everything around you.

The term *subtle body* is often used in esoteric teachings, but it is also a useful way to think about your own energetic systems, especially if this way of thinking is somewhat new to you. You have a physical body that you care for on a daily basis. Even if you're not super health-conscious, you still make sure to eat, drink, and maintain some semblance of cleanliness and hygiene. This is taking care of your physical body. You might take things a step—or a dozen steps!—further, and exercise on a regular basis, eat or drink certain foods, make weekly visits to the masseuse, the spa, the gym, etc. When you fail to take proper care of your physical body, you will feel the repercussions. Perhaps not immediately, but keep in mind you will always have to live with the consequences of your actions.

The same applies to your subtle body, your energetic body, which you might not be able to see but need to take care of, nonetheless. If you haven't paid much attention to your energy, like anything else, start small. Be conscious of your thoughts. Consider the types of food you eat and see where there is room for improvement. If you have been sedentary for a long time—and spending eight or more hours a day in a cubicle certainly makes a sedentary lifestyle more than a little easy to come by—add a little bit of exercise in, in increments. If you've got an incredibly busy schedule already, you might be wondering how this is possible, but it could be something as simple as taking the stairs when you'd normally take the elevator, or using part of your lunch break to take a walk around the block. Perhaps you're already active but would like to be more so. If you live somewhat near your job, maybe commuting by bicycle a few days a week would be a good option.

Meditation is another great way to help raise your vibrations. It is very easy in this day and age to get caught up in work, family life, and spending time in front of the laptop, the TV, the iPad. Children need to be shuttled from school to activities, the house needs to be maintained, and, oh yeah, there's your job, where you spend the majority of your waking hours. And maybe you'd like to squeeze in a few hours of sleep. It is understandable why meditation might not seem like it should be high on the list of priorities, but even meditating for as little as 10 minutes can be beneficial. Meditation is a respite of sorts, though if you're new to it, sitting alone with your thoughts might at first seem more like torture. It is generally not encouraged in our culture to sit and be idle; people who do so are considered lazy, unproductive, a waste of space. This is yet another example of when looking to the way of the lion can be helpful, as lions spend as much as 20 hours a day sleeping. Not to say that you should do the exact same thing, but even setting aside a small chunk of time to sit quietly will drastically help improve your well-being.

Once you become more accustomed to meditating, and get used to just sitting and allowing your thoughts to flow through you, you will be able to use this practice virtually anywhere. In the beginning, it will be helpful to choose a quiet place, free from distractions. But after a while, you will find that you no longer need a quiet place in order to meditate. Being able to quiet your mind and just be still is a powerful tool that will help raise your energetic vibrations.

There is a time when most everyone will be able to feel their energy coursing through them, whether or not they think they believe in this sort of thing, and that is when you feel fear. Fear can be used in a manner that is advantageous. Fear does not have to cripple or prevent you from undertaking something that you'd like to do but are hesitant to because you're uncertain how it might turn out. The feeling of fear affects your vibrations. This can manifest in both positive and negative ways. To use it in a positive way, allow it to be a motivator. In doing so, you will be embracing your fears and learning how to work with it, as opposed to it working against you.

YOU MIGHT FIND yourself rolling your eyes when you come across terms like *vibrations* or *energy levels*. You might not believe in that metaphysical, esoteric stuff—the realm of the unseen. That is okay. It's not for everyone, and if it just seems like it's way beyond the scope of anything you'd be able to believe in, I'm happy to tell you that there are non-metaphysical explanations for much of this as well.

You may or may not be familiar with the book *The Biology of Belief* by Bruce Lipton. He suggests that our thoughts affect how our cells change. Our cells are changing all the time, and what you think—the vibrational energy produced by what you think—can dictate how these cells change. The book is truly fascinating and can help those of you who are more scientific-minded understand how thoughts and the power of attraction works.

It reminds me of a project I did in middle school for the science fair. I went to the garden center and bought two potted African violets. They were the same size, and had the same number of flowers and almost the same exact number of velvety green leaves. I put the pots on the window ledge over the kitchen sink where they'd have plenty of sun, and I made sure to water them. I treated both plans identically, except for five minutes each day. One at a time, I'd take each plant into the study, where I'd shut the door. I spoke kindly to plant A and played pleasant music for it. I told it that it was a good plant and that it was growing beautifully. I did this for five minutes. Then I returned it to its ledge and took plant B into the study. I played no music for plant B. I told it that it was ugly, that it would never amount to anything, that it was basically a worthless piece of crap. I did this for five minutes, and then returned that plant back to the ledge.

I did this for a month, and at the end of the month, the results were startling. Plant A continued to flourish, an explosion of vibrant purple blossoms. Offshoots of new leaves were pushing through, and the plant was going to have to be repotted soon. Plant B, on the other hand, while not wilted, exactly, had few flowers, a number of dead spots on its leaves, and overall looked stunted and unhealthy. I'm not saying that you need to go out and talk to plants, but take my word for it: What you think and say matters. If you are constantly barraging yourself with doubtful, self-defeating talk, it is going to have an impact. Would you rather be healthy and flourish, or withered and defeated?

IT CAN FEEL overwhelming to take on the task of raising your vibrational frequency. You might think you won't be able to, or that your spouse or neighbors will think you're strange. It might seem like it's just not worth the time, but try to set those feelings aside. If you're up against someone who thinks this is all just a bunch of metaphysical, pseudo-spiritual hoo-ha, gently remind them that though things like radio waves cannot actually be seen, there is no denying they exist. A magnet's pull is invisible but is there nonetheless. Same goes for gravity. There are many things we can't necessarily see with our eyes but still exist. This will be harder for some people to accept than others, and that is okay. Some people will be more receptive to it, have perhaps had an experience that allows them to be more open to the idea of energy and vibrational frequencies.

Another way of looking at it is that you are upgrading yourself, similar to the way you would a computer. And when you consider that we've been programmed from a very early age—go to college, get a good job, work hard, have a family, plan for retirement—it's easy to imagine yourself as a program that you can download new information to. And you can use this information in whatever way is going to be most beneficial to you, so you are, in effect, upgrading yourself.

Chapter 12

The Gift of the Present

Almost two years after I met Jason at the coffee shop, he was able to leave the cubicle and start his bike shop. We still go on rides every now and then and it's amazing to see the transformation he's gone through.

"It's completely changed the way I think about things," he told me, when I asked him some of the ways his life was different now that he wasn't trapped in the office. "I think I actually work more hours than I was putting it before, but I'm doing something I enjoy. I'm doing something where I'm in charge of myself. It seems so obvious now, but I never realized how important that is—to be able to be in control of your life like that. And it's funny; once I changed how I was thinking about things, all sorts of doors opened."

It might surprise you to discover the ways in which the universe will bestow things upon you. While it is tempting to want to plan everything out, to know ahead of time what the outcome is going to be, oftentimes you have to make the leap without being able to fully see where you're going to land.

I'm glad Jason was willing to share his story, because I think he's in a position that many of you might find yourselves in. Having a family that you are responsible for always makes things a little harder than if you were just doing it on your own, like I was. It's often far too tempting to think that, if you've got a spouse, a couple kids, and a mortgage, you've missed the boat and just have to settle for where you are now in life (as in, you made your bed and now you must lie in it).

"I think the hardest part was getting going," Jason told me. "And that's a lot like riding a bike. I like that biking has basically paralleled the process it takes to get out of the cubicle. It's not easy to stay balanced on a bike if you're at a standstill. It's not impossible, but it's difficult. You need momentum. Especially when you're doing things like trail riding, and you come to some technical stuff, like roots or a rock garden. You've got to have momentum to carry you through. If you don't, you're going to end up on your ass on the side of the trail."

I think that's a good way of looking at it. I'm not expert at mountain biking, but I've learned a thing or two on my rides with Jason, and the hardest part really is getting started. And when you're staring down the trail and it's overrun with roots or there's some rather large rocks you've got to navigate, it's tempting to put the brakes on or maybe abandon the whole thing altogether. This is not unlike the challenges you might come up against as you move away from the cubicle and out on your own. I know it was helpful for Jason to be able to relate his journey out of the cubicle to bike riding, and you might want to consider what things in your life you can draw similar parallels to.

AS YOU BECOME more practiced with being aware of your thoughts and feelings, you might notice an interesting thing happening: You are more deeply connected to the present moment. The practice of staying in the present is also known as mindfulness, and being able to stay in the present truly is one of the best gifts you can give to yourself.

We have all experienced being stuck in the past. Perhaps it is a failed relationship or a missed opportunity. You might find yourself going over and over in your head the different choices you could have made and the different outcomes that would have resulted in. While it is certainly true that you can learn from the past, it is nearly impossible to put those learned lessons into practice if you can't let go and move forward.

So how do you move forward? There are many ways to do this, and what works for one might not work for another. Or, what worked for you for a certain situation might not be cutting it in a different scenario. Being adaptable, and at the same time being gentle with yourself, will help you overcome any regret and pain you might be feeling because of your past. Replaying the event in your head again and again is generally not going to help you move forward and is instead only going to conjure up frustration and other negative emotions. Certainly allow yourself to feel the full range of emotions associated with whatever it is that is bothering you, but then try to let it go. This, of course, is easier said than done, but like anything else, it takes practice. Seeking out new opportunities or a different direction, and acquiring new skills are great ways to help get yourself into the present moment while at the same time building momentum for your future.

This brings us to the other end of the spectrum: Anxiety about the future can be just as debilitating as being stuck in the past. Uncertainty can be a very uncomfortable feeling, but it is a part of life. While we all have certain hopes and dreams and ways we'd like to see things turn out, needless worrying about what might or might not happen can be very draining and is not going to affect the outcome.

Another effective tool to keep yourself from dwelling on the past or stressing out about the future is to keep a journal. If that sounds a little too maudlin for your tastes, just see it as writing your thoughts and feelings down. It doesn't have to be contained within a notebook, if you'd like; use the back of receipts, cocktail napkins, the margins of this book. Jason used a little notebook he was able to carry around with him; doing so allowed him to keep it handy and refer back to it when he needed to. Writing down your thoughts can be cathartic; it can also be a way to acknowledge what you're thinking and feeling, and then be able to move on. Some people also appreciate having a written record, as it can be helpful to see how something they were struggling with a week ago, a month ago, two or three years ago, has been overcome and maybe even transformed them.

Centering yourself in the present also requires you to practice non-judgment. This can be very difficult, as we often don't realize how many judgments we make, every single day. We judge ourselves, our family, our friends, and strangers we pass on the street. Some of our judgments are automatic; they are from our subconscious and we're not even aware that we're making them. Being in the present and paying attention to our thoughts will help us pinpoint these automatic judgments and will allow an opportunity for examination.

What is a judgment, anyway? It's an opinion, based solely on your perception. Often, it serves to bolster you while putting down someone else. While this may make you feel good temporarily, the feeling will be fleeting. You will need to continue to pass judgment on people to try to regain the feeling, and in some cases you'll find that, in your mind, you simply don't measure up. Whether this is true or not doesn't matter; now, instead of that temporary good feeling, you're feeling only negativity. It is a vicious cycle—one that can be difficult to break free from, especially if you're not even aware that it is happening.

Because some of our judgments are automatic, we don't even give them that much thought. Perhaps a judgment you've been making for years was based on an experience you had a long time ago that is no longer relevant in your current situation. Or maybe you're making a judgment that you don't necessarily believe. You will likely be amazed at the number of judgments you make that you don't actually agree with.

EVERYONE WOULD LIKE to have some semblance of control over his or her life, but you can't control the past because it's already happened, and you can't control the future because it hasn't happened yet. So that leaves you with the present moment, where you can be in full control of your own actions and thoughts. Keep in mind this doesn't mean you can control how others react to whatever it is you're doing or thinking, but it is in the here and now that you are your ship's captain. You might be surprised to find that, within the present moment, there is usually very little to worry about or stress over. Realizing and embodying this is essentially unlocking the cage and giving the lion within you its freedom—the limitless possibilities of achievement and satisfaction.

Conclusion

I like this quote from legendary Beat author Jack Kerouac: "Because in the end, you won't remember the time you spent working in the office or mowing your lawn. Climb that goddamn mountain." To climb that mountain—to free yourself from that cage—you need momentum; you need drive and determination. And if this book has found its way into your hands and you've made it to the end, then clearly you already have some momentum; the process for you has already begun.

Energy is not static. What you put out there, you will get back. It can be difficult to have trust in the universe, and to believe that it is going to provide what you need, but if you are willing to put in the effort, it will. This does not mean that you won't have trials to go through or that life won't be incredibly hard at certain points. It would've been easy for me to give up when I was arrested by the Secret Service, or when I was sued. I could have just thrown in the towel and got any job I could because I had serious debt I needed to start paying off. Things could have gone a number of ways, but if you stay in the present moment and trust that eventually things will work out how they're supposed to, your efforts will be rewarded.

Along the way, do what you can to help others. Embodying a spirit of altruism will empower both you and those you come in contact with. The positive energy you put out there by helping other people will reverberate, probably in more ways than you realize. Even something as simple as a smile or a few words of advice can go a long way. Sometimes, that is all a person needs for a bad day to suddenly be transformed into a good one.

GANDHI SAID, "LIVE as if you were to die tomorrow. Learn as if you were to live forever." James Dean's version is similar: "Dream as if you'll live forever. Live as if you'll die today." You can take the phrase *Live as if* and add whatever ending you'd like. You can customize it to your particular situation; tailor it as you see fit. Maybe you are still in the cubicle, not quite ready to make the full transition yet to doing what it really is you want. Yet you can still *live as if* you are a business owner, or an entrepreneur, or whatever it is that you are working toward. Living as if puts you in the mindset of already having, or being on your way to having, what it is you want to achieve. Sometimes we can't rush out and drop everything to undertake a new venture. Sometimes these things require planning, maybe even over the long term. Maybe you have a family or a mortgage, or both, or maybe you've got a mountain of school loans to pay back. Maybe you've got to take your plans a little slower than if you were single and debt-free. That doesn't mean you need to abandon your ideas, even if it feels like you're not at the point where you can actively work toward achieving them.

The thing is, you are. You might still be making the daily commute into the office every morning, but you will still be able to find moments when you can turn your attention and energies onto your own business or project. Remember: small steps. It can be difficult to be patient— to delay gratification. You've got this great idea and you just want to go after it, now. If you are able to do that, great. If not, that's great, too. And the majority of people will not be able to just drop what they have been doing and dedicate themselves fully to their new idea. It is so often a juggling act—a balancing act on a high, thin wire where you feel like there is no safety net and there is a giant crowd below, all eyes trained on you.

As you go through life, be powerful but relaxed. Know when to retract your claws and when they need to be out at full force. There is a lion that resides in each and every one of us, and it is just waiting for you to step out of your cubicle and allow it to roam free.

Made in the USA
San Bernardino, CA
15 June 2020

73311331R00066